D1461407

WITHDRAWN
FROM STOCK

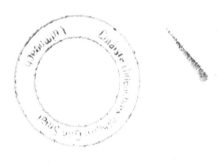

Alcohol, Drugs, and School-leavers

Alcohol, Drugs, and School-leavers

MARTIN A. PLANT
DAVID F. PECK
ELAINE SAMUEL

With the assistance
of Ray Stuart

Tavistock Publications

London and New York

First published in 1985 by
Tavistock Publications Ltd
11 New Fetter Lane,
London EC4P 4EE

Published in the USA by
Tavistock Publications
in association with Methuen, Inc.
29 West 35th Street
New York, NY 10001

© 1985 Martin A. Plant,
David F. Peck, and Elaine Samuel

Typeset by Keyset Composition,
Colchester, and printed in Great
Britain at the University Press,
Cambridge

*British Library Cataloguing in
Publication Data*

Plant, Martin A.
Alcohol, drugs and school-leavers.
1. Youth—Great Britain—Alcohol use
2. Youth—Great Britain—Drug use
I. Title   II. Peck, David F.
III. Samuel, Elaine
362.2'9'088054   HV5135

ISBN 0-422-78260-2

*Library of Congress Cataloging in
Publication Data*

Plant, Martin A.
Alcohol, drugs, and school-leavers.
Bibliography: p.
Includes indexes.
1. Youth—Great Britain—
Substance use—Longitudinal studies.
2. Dropouts—Great Britain—
Substance use—Longitudinal studies.
I. Peck, David F. II. Samuel, Elaine.
III. Stuart, Ray. IV. Title.
HV4999.Y68P57   1985   362.2'9   85-1475
ISBN 0-422-78260-2

'Although an ounce of prevention may be worth a pound of cure, we have not been able to provide a gram of either for youthful drinking problems.'
(Smart 1979b: 229)

This book is dedicated to:
Moira and Emma (M. A. P.)
Ailsa, Alex, and Claire (D. F. P.)
and to Stanley and Aaron (E. S.)

Contents

Special Acknowledgement

The authors wish to acknowledge the enormous contribution that was made to the project upon which this book was based by their friend and colleague Mrs Ray Stuart. It is in large measure due to her help that the three waves of fieldwork and the 'diplomacy' involved in this exercise were accomplished so successfully.

M. A. P.
D. F. P.
E. S.

Special Acknowledgement

Acknowledgements

The authors acknowledge advice and support, in designing and implementing this study and in compiling this book, from the following people.

The late Dr David L. Davies of the Alcohol Education Centre who was an adviser and a friend; Mr W. Semple, Director of the Lothian Region Education Department; Professor R. E. Kendell of the Department of Psychiatry, University of Edinburgh; Dr Norman Kreitman, Director of the MRC Unit for Epidemiological Studies in Psychiatry, Edinburgh University; Professor Griffith Edwards, Director, Addiction Research Unit, London; Professor Gustav Jahoda and Dr John B. Davies of the Department of Psychology, and Dr Philip Aitken of the Department of Advertising, University of Strathclyde; Dr Jussi Simpura of the Social Research Institute of Alcohol Studies, Helsinki; Mr Ralph McGuire of the Department of Psychiatry, and Mr John Duffy of the Department of Statistics, University of Edinburgh, are thanked for advice concerning statistical analysis. The study's progress and documentation has been aided by the comments and advice of many people. These involve other colleagues in the Alcohol Research Group, Edinburgh, together with participants at the Scottish Alcohol Problems Research Symposia and the Alcohol Epidemiology Section of the International Council on Alcohol and the Addictions.

Mr Ian Young of the Scottish Health Education Group and Ms Pamela Gillies of the Department of Community Health at Nottingham University are thanked for supplying some of the information that is cited in this book. The third wave of data collection was accomplished largely because of the enthusiasm and dedication of the interviewers.

Special thanks go to the following interviewers: Elizabeth Brown, Malcolm Bruce, Mayoor Cairns, John Clark, Douglas Dalgleish, Miranda Harvey, Vera Power, Simon Taylor, and C. S. Lindsay

Young. Thanks go to the following interviewers: Ron Bowers, Colin Brydon, Susan Chase, Ellen French, Susan Hogan, Colin Hunter, Fanchea Kelly, Ruth MacAuley, Ted Myers, Joyce Nicol, Ian Rankin, Hazel Robertson, Ian Sesnan, Pat Straw, Valerie Waldron, and Patrick Winckles.

The typing and a considerable amount of administrative work were carried out at astounding speed by Mrs Marjory Dodd, Mrs Elma Macdonald, Mrs Valerie Mannings, Mrs Janis Nicol, and Mrs Patricia Rose.

The study from which this book is based was funded by a grant from the Chief Scientist Office of the Scottish Home and Health Department. Additional financial support was generously provided by the Scotch Whisky Association and by the Medical Council on Alcoholism.

The greatest debt is due to the subjects of this study. These young men and women overwhelmingly co-operated with this venture with patience and enthusiasm. In so doing they provided a glimpse of part of their lives.

Some of the material in Chapter 3 of this book has appeared in other publications. Acknowledgements of copyright and thanks for permission to cite are made to the following:

Junction Books for Plant, M. A. (1982) Drinking Habits. In M. A. Plant (ed.) *Drinking and Problem Drinking*, 91–6.

British Journal of Addiction for Plant, M. A., Peck, D. F., and Stuart, R. (1982) Self-Reported Drinking Habits and Alcohol-Related Consequences amongst a Cohort of Scottish Teenagers. 77: 75–90; and for Plant, M. A., Peck, D. F., and Stuart, R. (1984) The Correlates of Serious Alcohol-Related Consequences and Illicit Drug Use Amongst a Cohort of Scottish Teenagers. 79: 197–200.

1 Young People, Alcohol, Tobacco, and Illicit Drugs

This book is about a group of young people whose use of alcohol and other psychoactive (mind-altering) drugs was followed up for four years. The research upon which this book is based was initiated for two main reasons. The first of these relates to widespread concern about the upsurge of excessive or inappropriate drug use amongst young people. Central to this concern has been evidence of increasingly widespread alcohol misuse involving people under the age of 21. In addition both tobacco smoking and the use of illicit substances such as glues, solvents, cannabis, and opiates have received widespread publicity. During the past twenty years the focus of public attention has periodically switched from one youthful drug fashion to the next. Pep pills gave way to cannabis and LSD, which gave way to alcohol, then later to glue sniffing and thence to heroin. Such swings of concern have been influenced by evidence of new drug fashions, but have overemphasized and often sensationalized the likely patterns of drug use amongst young people in the community. Public alarm has accompanied a wideranging, yet sadly ineffective, set of responses. Some of these have been prompted by the widespread belief that young people are both especially likely to misuse drugs and are also exceptionally vulnerable to their potential ill effects.

Many debates about the misuse of alcohol, tobacco, and illicit drugs have culminated in the plea for better health education in order to lay 'the facts' before young people and so enable them to behave in a more enlightened, rational, and safe manner. The widespread faith in education as a means of preventing drug problems, and in the case of this study, particularly of alcohol problems, prompted the second aim of this research project which relates to the effectiveness of alcohol education. The purpose and methods of this study are described in the following chapter. Even so, it is appropriate to indicate at this stage what this book is about. Its central focus is the pattern of alcohol use amongst 'normal' young people from a variety of backgrounds. These individuals are examined before and after leaving school in order to illuminate some of the influences upon the use and misuse of alcohol, as well as of tobacco and illicit drugs. It is hoped that this exercise will be of value to readers who, for whatever reasons, wish to consider the social and psychological processes associated with the acquisition and adoption of youthful drinking, smoking, and illicit drug taking. It is also hoped that this book will be helpful to those considering whether to provide health education in this field. This research project was originally conceived as being solely an 'alcohol study'. Alcohol remains the major focus. In spite of this, for empirical reasons clarified in the following chapters, and because of a surge of public interest which occurred during the course of this investigation, illicit drug use is also considered, together with tobacco smoking.

Before embarking upon a brief review of recent trends in youthful use and misuse of legal and illegal drugs, it is important to acknowledge that such misuse is not, and never has been, the sole prerogative of young people. The average age of those admitted as in-patients to psychiatric hospitals for alcohol dependence is over 40. The over-whelming majority of those dependent upon tobacco are middle-aged and elderly. In fact young people in the United Kingdom are *less* likely to smoke tobacco than are their parents. In addition most of those receiving prescriptions for the so-called 'benzodiazepines' (such as Valium, Librium, and Ativan) are also middle-aged and elderly. Approximately one million people in the United Kingdom receive prescriptions for benzodiazepines. In the 1983 *Annual Report* of the Medical Research Council it was noted that: 'about 10 per cent of those patients taking benzodiazepines develop dependence' (Medical Research Council 1983: 24).

This problem, related to drugs which have hitherto been widely regarded as relatively 'safe', follows earlier evidence of extensive problems amongst middle-aged and elderly people receiving amphetamines and barbiturates on prescription. Fatal drug overdoses are most common not among the young but amongst the elderly. In spite of this catalogue of woes, disproportionate attention has been accorded to the drug misuse of young people. Concern is far from unfounded but has sometimes been strangely blinkered in relation to comparable misuse evident amongst older people.

The use of mind-altering drugs has been increasing world-wide. Both licit and illicit substances are used recreationally (for fun) more than ever before. Two important factors are amongst many reasons for this. The first relates to the unparalleled availability of an ever-increasing variety of legal and illegal drugs. The services of indigent and diligent peasants, efficient manufacturers, and fast international travel have combined to invent, produce, and speedily distribute an unprecedented array of depressants, stimulants, and hallucinogens. The second impetus to the demand for drugs has been the falling price of many commodities compared to what the average consumer is able to afford.

The use of alcohol, tobacco, and illicit drugs is motivated by many different influences. These include a wish to experiment with or to enjoy the often pleasant effects of specific drugs and peer pressure to imbibe them. Social, cultural, and environmental factors, together with the individual traits (personality, intelligence, sex, age) of the potential user or users combine with biological, political, economic, and historical factors. It follows that so many influences impinge upon drug use and thereby misuse that no single or simple remedy has yet emerged, or could emerge, as a solution to drug problems.

Social responses have been largely fragmented. There has been a proliferation of agencies offering help to those with problems related to alcohol, illicit and prescribed drugs, and, occasionally, tobacco. Considerable sums of public money continue to be spent on research and education. Even so, most of the evidence related to the results of these responses is depressing. Only modest gains have been apparent in most fields of response. Most forms of drug use and misuse have simply continued to increase.

ALCOHOL

Alcohol is by far the most widely used recreational psychoactive drug. Over 90 per cent of adults in Britain and over 60 per cent of those in Eire and in Northern Ireland drink alcohol, if only occasionally. Approximately 750,000 people are engaged in the production and distribution of alcoholic beverages in the United Kingdom, and in the year preceding 31 March, 1984 the drink trade produced approximately £5,963,800,000 in revenue for the government. Between 1950 and 1978 per capita alcohol consumption in the United Kingdom virtually doubled. During the same period the 'real price' of alcoholic

4 Alcohol, Drugs, and School-leavers

beverages, that is price related to what people can afford to spend, roughly halved. Alcohol consumption has soared dramatically in most countries where records are available. In fact, the level of alcohol consumption in the United Kingdom is not high by international standards. The average French adult consumes more than twice as much alcohol each year as does the average Briton. Per capita alcohol consumption is higher in most Western and East European countries than it is in the United Kingdom. Only the Scandinavians amongst Britain's nearest neighbours drink less per capita than do the British. The United Kingdom is not remarkable in relation to its level of alcohol consumption. Even so, in common with other countries, an enormous proliferation of alcohol-related problems has been noted in the United Kingdom in association with the general increase in the level of alcohol consumption. These problems include drunken driving and public drunkenness offences, marital discord and child abuse, alcohol dependence, and liver cirrhosis. While there does not appear to be a neat mathematical formula, it is clear that whenever the level of alcohol use in a given country goes up, so does the level of alcohol misuse. Though varying in both type and extent in different settings, this misuse extends far beyond what is conventionally construed as alcohol dependence. Large numbers of people are harmed by such misuse, either directly or indirectly. Recent research has shown that over a quarter of those killed on the roads in England and Wales, and over half of their counterparts in Scotland, have blood alcohol levels in excess of the legal limit for drinking of 80 mg/100 ml (Sabey and Staughton 1980). Between 1970 and 1982 rates of death from chronic liver cirrhosis and disease in the United Kingdom rose by 60 per cent. The British rate of first admission to psychiatric hospitals for alcohol dependence and alcoholic psychosis rose between 1970 and 1977 by 75 per cent. Between 1970 and 1980 the United Kingdom rate of convictions for drunkenness rose by roughly a quarter. During the same period the British rate of convictions for drunken driving more than doubled. Such indicators are far from perfect. Some reflect the provision of services or other factors (such as the growth in car ownership). Even so, in the United Kingdom as elsewhere, the rates of liver cirrhosis mortality and drunkenness convictions clearly show that alcohol misuse has reached major proportions.

As alcohol consumption and alcohol misuse have reached higher levels, concern has become focused upon several subgroups within the population not hitherto regarded as particularly vulnerable to alcohol problems. Both women and young people have become, rightly or wrongly, the two primary targets of such interest. Widespread media coverage has highlighted issues such as teenage drunkenness, underage drinking, teenage 'alcoholism' and the alleged secret tippling of bored or distressed housewives. Drinking during pregnancy has been identified as a possible cause of birth abnormalities and is the subject of much attention (Plant, M. L. 1985).

The world recession has been accompanied by a fall in alcohol consumption and alcohol-related problems in some countries. Between 1979 and 1982 annual alcohol consumption per head of population in the United Kingdom declined from 13.7 pints of pure alcohol to 12.3 pints. Broadly similar falls in alcohol consumption have been noted in other countries such as the USA and France. In spite of this, no uniform pattern has been evident. In some countries, such as the USSR, Finland, Australia, and Canada, alcohol consumption has been virtually stable during this period while in others, such as East Germany, Peru, and South Africa, alcohol consumption has risen.

In Britain rates of first admissions to psychiatric hospitals for alcohol dependence and alcoholic psychosis declined between 1977 and 1982. Between 1980 and 1982 United Kingdom drunkenness convictions also declined slightly. In 1981 drunken driving convictions in Britain were lower than in the previous year, though this can hardly be regarded as 'a trend'.

It has been clear for a considerable time that frequent heavy drinking is particularly commonplace amongst young single people. A survey of Scottish drinking habits conducted during 1972 and published four years later indicated that 30 per cent of all the alcohol reportedly consumed by a representative sample of adults was imbibed by a mere 3 per cent of those interviewed. These prodigious drinkers were young male manual workers in their teens and twenties (Dight 1976). Other surveys in Britain, North America, and elsewhere have reached similar conclusions. Young people do a lot of drinking. Within the United Kingdom the heaviest drinkers are mainly young and unmarried. Even so, as already noted, most of those who seek help for alcohol dependence are not so young: they are mainly in their late thirties, forties, or fifties. Alcohol dependence usually takes several years to develop. However, alcohol misuse does not necessarily involve dependence, and there is abundant evidence that some alcohol-related problems have increased greatly amongst young people.

The above debate has been couched in the language of alcohol dependence. In fact alcohol misuse amongst the young seldom involves such dependence. For example, Flint (1974) has commented:

'There are indications from a variety of sources that drinking of alcohol among teenagers is increasing. This increased likelihood of early contact with alcohol must inevitably put more teenagers at risk of becoming physically and psychologically dependent upon, and addicted to, alcohol. Not only do various indicators of alcohol abuse suggest this increase but there is evidence that young problem drinkers are likely to develop into alcoholics more quickly than adults and that the earlier the onset of alcohol abuse, the poorer the prognosis.'

(Flint 1974: 1)

In 1980 fewer than 5 per cent of those admitted to Scottish psychiatric hospitals for alcohol dependence were aged 24 or under. Similarly only very few of those in Britain who were recorded as dying from liver cirrhosis are aged 25 or less (Latcham 1984). Both alcohol dependence and alcohol-related liver cirrhosis take time to evolve. Young people may be developing towards both of these conditions but are unlikely to come to the attention of agencies until they are older. In spite of this young people frequently come to the attention of law enforcement agencies. In 1962 11.5 per cent of males, and 6.5 per cent of females in England and Wales who were convicted of drunkenness were under the age of 21. The comparable Scottish figures were 7.1 per cent and 3.2 per cent.

By 1979, the year when the study described in this book began, this pattern had changed considerably. Amongst those convicted of drunkenness in England and Wales 21.3 per cent of males and 15.6 per cent of females were under the age of 21. The comparable Scottish figures were 9.8 per cent and 8.9 per cent. Except, oddly, amongst Scottish males, there had been a marked increase in the proportion of drunkenness offenders who were over 21.

The rise in the proportion of drunkenness offences involving young people is not solely, or even substantially, attributable to demographic changes. Between 1961 and 1981 the proportion of the United Kingdom population aged 15 to 19 increased only very slightly. In 1979 8.1 per cent of the United Kingdom population were in the 15 to 19 age group. Clearly the number of young drunkenness offenders in England

and Wales in that year was disproportionate to the relative size of this age group. The corresponding proportion of young people in Scotland amongst drunkenness offenders was, however, broadly in line with their numbers in the population (*Abstract of Statistics* 1984: 10–12). It is emphasized that this apparent difference may be to some extent attributable to the fact that drunkenness legislation in Scotland is not the same as in England and Wales. This has been noted elsewhere (Kilich and Plant 1981, 1982).

Young people are a high-risk group in relation to drunken driving (Myers 1982; Ross 1984). Between 1963 and 1981 the proportion of those in Scotland convicted of drunken driving who were over the age of 21 rose from 4 per cent to 11 per cent (Scottish Home and Health Department 1984). It must be noted that this rise probably indicates the extent of youthful access to motor vehicles rather than any particular change in drinking habits. Wilson (1980b) has suggested that alcohol consumption in Scotland may have been relatively stable throughout much of this period. It has recently been declining.

Just as drinking patterns vary amongst different age groups, they do appear to differ in different parts of Britain. It is well documented that rates of officially recorded alcohol-related problems vary considerably between different regions. These problems include drunkenness crimes, liver cirrhosis deaths, and hospital admissions for alcohol dependence. Such rates are generally higher in Scotland and the north of England than they are further south. This view has been supported by several authors (Plant and Pirie 1979; Davies 1982; Haskey, Balarajan, and Donnan 1983). These variations are depicted by *Figure 1* (Kilich and Plant 1981, 1982). It has been widely assumed that the reason for this variation is simply that people in the north of Britain drink more heavily than they do elsewhere. In fact evidence on this topic is conflicting. One survey conducted in 1978 indicated that while 'heavy drinking' was more commonplace in the north than in the south, this did not mirror regional rates of alcohol-related problems very closely (Office of Population Censuses and Surveys 1980). More recent evidence has suggested that drinking habits in Scotland differ only very slightly from those in England and Wales. In spite of this the Scots may have a marginally more 'concentrated' style of drinking than their southern counterparts (Wilson 1980a, 1980b). It is also possible that at least some of the differences indicated by *Figure 1* are reflections, not of 'real' differences but rather of variations in 'official' recording procedures (Latcham *et al.* 1984; Crawford *et al.* 1984).

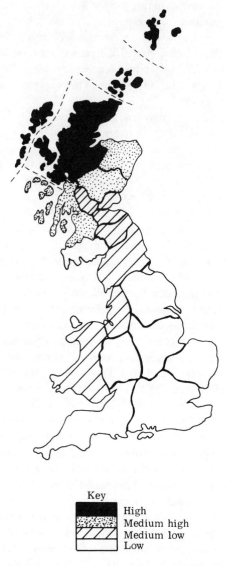

Key

■ High
▨ Medium high
▨ Medium low
□ Low

Figure 1. Rates of officially recorded alcohol-related problems in Britain

TOBACCO: THE GRIM REAPER

The drug responsible for the most widespread health damage is indisputably tobacco. At a conservative estimate 100,000 people per year die prematurely due to the effects of tobacco smoking in the United Kingdom alone. The link between smoking and ill health has only become evident since the 1950s. Several studies indicated a dramatic association between tobacco use and lung cancer. Since then research has revealed links between tobacco and a wide range of serious health problems. These include chronic bronchitis, emphysema, and diseases of the heart and circulatory system. In addition, women who smoke during pregnancy produce smaller offspring than do non-smokers and are more likely to experience miscarriages.

The Royal College of Physicians produced four major reports on smoking between 1962 and 1983. In the most recent of these the catastrophic scale of tobacco-related damage was graphically illustrated thus:

'Among 1,000 young male adults in England and Wales who smoke cigarettes on average about:
  1 will be murdered
  6 will be killed on the roads
  250 will be killed before their time by tobacco.'
(Royal College of Physicians 1983: 2)

Although the level of harm attributable to tobacco is almost incomprehensible in its enormity, some encouragement may be derived from consumption trends. Since 1956 the percentage of adult males in the United Kingdom who smoke has fallen from 75 to 50. Some recent evidence indicates that by 1982 the proportion of males who smoke had fallen to only 38 per cent. Tobacco use by women remained relatively stable during the period 1960–72, but declined from 41 per cent to 33 per cent between 1972 and 1982 (Royal College of Physicians 1983: 105–6).

Tobacco sales in the United Kingdom have been falling since 1974. This trend, together with the recent and considerable fall in the percentage of adults who smoke, is clearly good news. This is in sharp contrast with the evidence of accelerating levels of most other forms of drug use.

Teenagers are less likely than older people to smoke tobacco. Even so, approximately a quarter of those aged 15 to 16 have been shown to be 'regular smokers' (Office of Population Censuses and Surveys 1983). Evidence suggests that the level of smoking amongst young people of either sex has been diminishing and that only minor differences exist between the percentages of girls and boys who smoke.

There are considerable regional variations in smoking habits in Britain. A review by Bostock and Davies (1979) showed that between 1972 and 1976 a higher percentage of the population aged 16 or above in Scotland and the north of England smoked than in the south of England. One reason for this variation is the marked social-class imbalance that exists within Britain. Manual workers are more likely than non-manual workers to smoke. There are a higher proportion of the former in the north than in the more prosperous south. This latter difference is reflected by higher rates of tobacco-related deaths in the north of Britain. The United Kingdom has one of the highest rates of such deaths in the world, and the rate in Scotland is higher than that of the rest of the United Kingdom.

ILLICIT DRUGS

'Illicit drugs' are both substances the use of which is legal though generally disapproved (such as glues and solvents), and those whose production, possession, and distribution are proscribed by law. During the nineteenth century opium use was legal. Even so there was serious disquiet about the widespread and often harmful use of this drug in Britain (Berridge and Edwards 1981). In the twentieth century little interest in illicit drugs was displayed until the 1960s. Before then a limited amount of cocaine use in artistic and literary circles and amongst prostitutes and seamen had been alleged to occur. Also evident was the 'therapeutic dependence' of a few hundred opiate users. These were mainly doctors, dentists, and nurses who had access to morphine, and middle-aged or elderly people who had received morphine while undergoing medical treatment and had developed dependence in consequence. The Rolleston Committee which reported in 1926 noted that such individuals were a relatively stable group of people whose dependence was purely a medical problem. This laid the foundations of what has since been called the 'British System' of managing opiate dependence. It is characterized by the legal prescribing by doctors of opiates or of similar drugs for addicts.

By the 1960s a new situation had arisen. This has been described in detail elsewhere (e.g. Plant 1981a; Edwards and Busch 1981; Gossop

1982). An unprecedented wave of 'recreational' drug experimentation amongst young people occurred. Amphetamines (pep pills) were extensively stolen and used illicitly. The misuse of these drugs coincided with the rising popularity of cannabis, the use of which had hitherto been extremely limited. In addition by the mid-1960s the Home Office was recording a clear increase in heroin dependence. This was not confined, as morphine dependence had been, to 'therapeutic addicts'. Instead young people were using opiates and encouraging their peers to follow suit. By the early 1970s a national network of police drug squads had been established. Drug treatment clinics were set up during 1968 in order both to limit the supply of prescribed opiates and to provide help for those dependent upon these drugs. Neither new laws nor new clinics managed to reduce the scale of illicit drug use (Stimson and Oppenheimer 1982). Between 1962 and 1983 the annual number of narcotic drug addicts in the United Kingdom recorded by the Home Office rose from 532 to 5,079. The Home Office register of 'addicts' is of only limited value. Most opiate users prefer to obtain heroin through illicit sources than to attend clinics. Few British clinics do in fact prescribe heroin; most use an alternative drug, Methadone. Some do not prescribe drugs at all. The Advisory Council on the Misuse of Drugs suggested in 1982 that a more realistic estimate of the possible number of drug users in the United Kingdom was 40,000 (Advisory Council on the Misuse of Drugs 1982).

In 1945 only four cannabis offences were recorded, together with 206 for opium, and 20 related to manufactured drugs. By the late 1960s over 10,000 drug convictions were recorded annually. Between 1973 and 1983 the number of persons convicted annually for drug offences rose from 14,977 to 23,341. Roughly three-quarters of all drug convictions relate to cannabis. The rest mainly relate to amphetamines, heroin, cocaine, dipipanone (Diconal), Methadone, and lysergic acid diethyl-amide (LSD).

Most drug offenders are young and male. In 1982, 88 per cent of those convicted or cautioned for drug offences were males and in 1983, 56 per cent of offenders were under the age of 25. Recorded narcotic addicts are also mainly young. In 1983, 19 per cent were under 25 years of age and a further 27 per cent were aged 25 to 29. During the same year 29 per cent of recorded narcotic addicts were females.

Official figures give a highly selective and unrepresentative impression of illicit drug use. Most recreational drug use is discreet and never comes to light. Surveys have shown that amongst secondary-school pupils and college and university students illicit drug use is widespread and has almost certainly been increasing. A recent national sample survey indicated that between 13 and 28 per cent of young people aged 15 to 21 in different areas of Britain had used cannabis at some time (NOP Market Research Ltd 1982).

Until recently concern about illicit drug use was higher in the south of England than it was in Scotland. During the period covered by this study (1979–83) the number of 'addicts' in Scotland who were recorded by the Home Office at the end of each year rose from 107 to 283, an increase of 160 per cent. Elsewhere in the United Kingdom addict notifications rose by only 87 per cent. An Edinburgh general practitioner has stated that amongst 18,000 patients 162 were known to have used heroin intravenously (Robertson 1985).

All British surveys have indicated that males are more likely than females to use illicit drugs. Even so, some have shown that this difference is not great. Surveys have uniformly shown that illicit drug use is commonplace amongst young people, particularly those in their teens and twenties. Such use has not been confined to any specific subgroup, although some evidence has indicated that those from deprived backgrounds, or with the lowest social status, are most likely to use a wide range of drugs or to inject drugs. Since the 1960s it has been apparent that most illicit drug use (like most alcohol use) is casual and does not lead to dependence or to conspicuous harm. A minority of those who have taken illicit drugs are regular users. These individuals frequently use not one, but a whole range of substances. Such polydrug use characterizes those most deeply involved with the lifestyle of the drug scene and is often accompanied by heavy alcohol and tobacco use.

Surveys have shown most illicit drug use to be confined to teenagers or to older age groups. Some use by younger people has been noted, in particular with relation to the inhalation of glues and solvents. During the marked increase of illicit drug use noted at the beginning of the 1980s considerable media attention was focused on reportedly widespread glue sniffing amongst primary-school children and sometimes even amongst younger children. Some community workers, clinicians, and researchers have reported that in many areas opiate use is rapidly becoming far more widespread amongst those in their mid teens and even younger. It was also noted that some of the new opiate users were either smoking heroin or heating it and inhaling its fumes. The latter practice, known as 'chasing the dragon', is not new but appears to have gained popularity.

Speculation was voiced at the possible link between these trends and high and increasing levels of unemployment amongst school-leavers. At the same time public spending cuts were reducing the number of Customs and Excise officers available to stem the inflow of illicit drugs (through ports and airports) into Britain.

DISCUSSION

Public debate about drug use and misuse is stubbornly dogged by myths and stereotypes. It is of course optimistic to suppose that public policy on drugs will ever be wholly rational. In spite of this, constructive responses are not helped by sensationalized media coverage or by the heightening of public fears which are out of all proportion to the real scale of the problem. At the time of writing, some British tabloid newspapers give huge coverage to deaths associated with youthful solvent and heroin use which are fortunately extremely rare. The same newspapers virtually ignore the harm associated with tobacco and may publish cigarette advertisements side by side with stories of the horrors of glue sniffing. Social problems do warrant emotion, concern, and commitment. They also need a sense of balance and responsibility.

This chapter has attempted to set the rest of this book into the broader context of widespread drug use. The subjects of this book were a 'normal' group of young people who were examined not because they were freaks or particularly vulnerable, but simply because they were normal.

During 1980, 267 people in the 15–19 age group died in Scotland. Seven of these deaths were recorded as somehow drug related. Over 200 of the remainder were due to road accidents (Registrar General Scotland 1982). Available evidence suggests that many of the latter were alcohol related (Sabey and Staughton 1980). Even with this major caveat these and other figures do not conform to the popular assumption that youthful drug dependence is rife or that large numbers of young people die each year from the effects of illicit drug use. It is hoped that the research described in this book will help to provide at least a crude and limited picture of the use of alcohol and other drugs by a group of young people. In addition it is hoped that some of the important empirical and policy issues relating to youthful substance use will be highlighted with reference both to this new study and to the now vast literature on the use and misuse of drugs by young people.

2 The Study

During recent years there has been great concern about, and interest in, the drinking habits and alcohol-related problems of teenagers. This has been manifested by the production of a series of health education aids for young people. In addition, several studies have examined the attitudes to drinking and the drinking behaviour of young people (e.g. Jahoda and Crammond 1972; Davies and Stacey 1972; O'Connor 1978; Hawker 1978; Aitken 1978).

One reason for the interest in the alcohol-related behaviour and attitudes of teenagers is the growing evidence that this section of the population has been drinking more and encountering more alcohol-related problems. Apart from any intrinsic interest in teenagers in relation to alcohol use, it has long been assumed that young people are an important target group for health education activities. This view reflects the belief that if the young are educated about alcohol and drinking they will subsequently be less likely to drink harmfully (Grant 1982a). In fact, the relationship between youthful attitudes to alcohol and subsequent alcohol-related behaviour is unclear.

There appear to be two distinct problems. The first is the general question of whether the knowledge, attitudes, and behaviour (concerning alcohol) of school-leavers do in fact relate to their drinking habits after they leave school and come under the influence of a new peer group. This question clearly merits detailed enquiry; a positive finding should help indicate which components of the school-leavers' 'awareness' of alcohol have the greater association with subsequent behaviour and hence should provide guidance on educational objectives, while a negative result would suggest various possibilities, of which one is that health education efforts would be better directed to an earlier or to a later stage in life.

The second and subsidiary question concerns how far school-based education concerning alcohol is effective in modifying the views of teenage pupils. For present purposes this problem will be defined in terms of the changes in alcohol use during the final year at school in the context of health education programmes. In practice it is not always easy to specify whether teaching has or has not been given on this topic, or what its content has been, but a simple categorization appears to be feasible. By a consideration of a variety of schools the short-term efficacy of different programmes can be compared. Additionally, by linking this component of the project with the follow-up study it may also be possible to assess whether 'views' inculcated by the school have the same predictive power as similar views held by pupils who have not received any specific teaching.

This book describes a research project which was implemented to achieve the following aims:

(1) To determine whether the knowledge, attitudes, and behaviour concerning alcohol among school-leavers predict subsequent alcohol-related behaviour.

(2) To find out whether educational programmes during the final year of compulsory school attendance (age 15–16) meet their objectives in the short term, and have any discernible effect on alcohol-related behaviour after the teenager has left school.

The first of these is the *primary component*. The *secondary component*, concerning health education in schools, is logically separated.

Alcohol is not the only drug whose misuse by young people is of interest. As noted in Chapter 1, tobacco and illicit drugs are major focuses for public concern. Available evidence indicates that there is frequently an association between alcohol consumption by young people and their use of tobacco and illicit drugs (such as cannabis, heroin, glues, and solvents). Accordingly it was decided to broaden the scope of this investigation by examining the use of these substances by the study group as well as their drinking habits.

THE STUDY AREA

This study was carried out in the Lothian Region which is in the south-east of Scotland and is focused upon the capital city of Edinburgh. The city itself has a population of approximately 425,000 and the surrounding region contains approximately 300,000 more people. Edinburgh is a major banking, educational, and commercial centre. Several manufacturing interests are located in the vicinity. These include brewing and distilling, micro-electronics, coal mining, and agriculture. The socio-economic composition of the Lothian Region is fairly close to that of Great Britain as a whole. Approximately 46 per cent of those in Lothian live in households headed by a non-manual worker, compared with 43 per cent of those in Britain as a whole.

DESIGN

Since this study was concerned with relationships between variables over time, a longitudinal design was adopted. The primary component of the study required a comparison between data collected at the

Table 1 The design of the study

schools	t1	t2	t3
1			
2			
3			
4			
5			

t1 = survey at beginning of last compulsory year of school attendance
t2 = survey later in last compulsory year of school attendance
t3 = follow-up after leaving school
t1 − t2 = consistency check of results of first wave of data collection
t1 − t3 = longer-term correlation between attitudes to, and knowledge of, drinking and subsequent alcohol-related behaviour

beginning of the last compulsory year of school (t1) and follow-up data (t3). In addition an intermediate wave of data (t2) was collected as a reliability check and in order to ascertain whether or not alcohol education produced any changes within the final year's compulsory schooling.

METHOD

The subjects of this study were 15- and 16-year-old pupils attending five secondary schools either in Edinburgh or in the surrounding Lothian Region. The method adopted was to give self-administered questionnaires to pupils at the beginning of their final year and to repeat this procedure for all those still at school towards the end of that academic year. A minority of pupils in fact left school at the end of the autumn term during that year. These were not given the second questionnaire. Subsequently, all of the original respondents were sought for reinterview three years after initial data collection by trained interviewers using a standardized interview schedule.

The five schools used in this study were chosen in order to yield at least 1,000 pupils in the relevant age group. Four of these were state schools administered by Lothian Region Education Department. The fifth was an independent school. This selection was made to ensure that the pupils included in the study reflected the local balance between independent and state education. In the Lothian Region as a whole, approximately 8 per cent of secondary-school pupils attended independent schools during the study period. The state schools were chosen by systematic random selection from an alphabetical list of all of the secondary schools administered by the Lothian Region Education Department. The single independent school was chosen because it was able to provide the necessary 'quota' of at least forty male and forty female students aged either 15 or 16. The co-operation of the teaching staff at each school was secured by an initial letter of explanation and enquiry from the first author followed by one or several meetings between the first author and head teachers/rectors, together with other members of each school's teaching staff.

Initial overtures secured the full co-operation of two state schools and the single independent school. Head teachers at the other two state schools declined to accept the proposed method of obtaining parental consent for pupils to participate in the study. This method, and the objections raised in relation to it, are described below. Two substitute state schools of almost identical size to those excluded were successfully brought into the study. The four state schools finally involved in this research all contained pupils from a broad social spectrum. These, together with the independent school, certainly included pupils from virtually all the social and geographical backgrounds within the Lothian Region.

Arrangements were made for all fourth-year pupils in each of the five schools to be enlisted in the study group. Each pupil was given a duplicated letter to his/her parents. This briefly explained the aims and scope of the study and provided a reassurance of its confidentiality. Parents *not* wishing their children to participate were requested to complete a form which was to be returned to the relevant head teacher. This procedure for 'contracting out' of the study was adopted since it was thought that a considerable percentage of parents would fail, due to lack of motivation, to complete a form indicating that they *did* consent to their children participating in the study. There is some evidence to support this view. For example in an American follow-up study of high-school pupils, only 668 out of 1,126 parents approached (59.3 per cent) consented to their children's participation in a broadly comparable study (Jessor and Jessor 1978).

The two head teachers who refused to co-operate with the project did so because they objected to this method. Both stated that in their view (or in one case in the view of the school's Parent Teacher Association) only pupils whose parents actively consented should be included in the study.

As noted above, initial data were elicited by a standardized self-completed questionnaire. Full details of this instrument are provided in Appendix 1. The questionnaire elicited information on the following subjects: 1) biographical details; 2) alcohol consumption; 3) alcohol-related consequences; 4) attitudes to alcohol use and misuse; 5) tobacco smoking; 6) illicit drug use.

Pre-testing and Piloting

The questions included in the initial version of the questionnaire were pre-tested in May, 1979 upon three pupils (two boys and a girl) attending a comprehensive school not included in the main study group. Data were collected by the first author administering the questions verbally, not by self-completion. At the end of each interview (which took roughly 30 minutes to complete) the respondent was asked whether he or she had understood each of the questions clearly and to make suggestions to improve the design and scope of the interview. These three trial interviews revealed no major difficulties and each led to modifications or additions that were introduced for the formal piloting of the questionnaire.

The complete data collection procedure was piloted in June, 1979 with a group of thirty-eight pupils who were attending the same school.

On this occasion data were obtained by each respondent filling in the standardized questionnaire. The school's rector (head teacher) and his colleagues permitted the first author to have access to a mixed-sex class of pupils of widely varied academic ability for a one-hour period. A brief verbal explanation of the nature and purpose of the questionnaire was given and each pupil was instructed to complete it without discussion with classmates. No major problems were encountered and all thirty-eight pupils were able to complete their questionnaires in 30 to 35 minutes.

The pilot data collection showed that the questionnaire was largely satisfactory. Only two minor modifications seemed to be necessary before it could be used for the main initial fieldwork. All thirty-eight respondents filled in the questionnaire adequately. In addition, the respondents were asked to indicate whether or not they were prepared to co-operate with follow-up interviews three years later. Twenty-nine agreed and nine did not agree to do so. Thirty-six of the thirty-eight provided their home addresses in full. In addition, twenty-four provided one additional address; of these, twenty also provided a second additional address which could, if necessary, be used to facilitate contact for follow-up interviews.

On this basis it appeared that more than three-quarters of those interviewed in the main fieldwork would, in principle, agree to co-operate with a follow-up interview. Even more encouraging, it appeared that virtually all would be prepared to provide at least one address through which an attempt could be made to recontact them in three years' time. From a projection of the results of the pilot interviews to the planned interviews of 1,000 pupils, the follow-up prospects were as shown in *Table 2*.

On the basis of these results it was decided that the prospects for follow-up might be enhanced by attempting to recontact *all* respondents who provided one or more addresses (94.7 per cent). In order to maximize the chances of successful follow-up, it was decided not to ask respondents whether or not they wanted to co-operate, but to let them make that decision if they were successfully traced by interviewers three years after their initial interviews. This decision was justified on the grounds that it theoretically increased the percentage of possible respondents from 76.3 to 94.7. In addition, this approach was deemed ethical since, if approached for reinterview at a later date, each respondent would be able to refuse to co-operate if he or she chose to do so.

The timetable of the complete study is shown in *Table 3*.

Table 2 Response to pilot survey and projected results

response	pilot interviews n 38	projected results for n 1,000	
		n	%
agree to follow-up	29	763	76.3
not agree to follow-up	9	237	23.7
provide own address	36	947	94.7
not provide own address	2	53	5.3
provide second address	24	631	63.1
provide third address	20	526	52.6

Table 3 Timetable of fieldwork

1. *May, 1979*
    Pre-testing initial self-completed questionnaire with three respondents.
2. *June, 1979*
    Piloting questionnaire with 38 respondents.
3. *November, 1979–February, 1980*
    Initial wave of data collection with 1,036 respondents.
4. *March–April, 1980*
    Second wave of data collection with 870 respondents.
5. *January, 1983*
    Pre-testing interview schedule with 5 respondents.
6. *February, 1983*
    Piloting revised interview schedule with 20 respondents.
7. *March–September, 1983*
    Third wave of data collection involving all 1,036 respondents. A total of 957 (92.4%) were successfully reinterviewed.

3 The Study Group

This chapter describes the results of the first of the three phases of this study. Statistical analysis has been kept to a minimum throughout this book. Even so, it has not been dispensed with entirely.

The initial fieldwork for this study was carried out between 14 November, 1979 and 11 February, 1980. Data collection avoided the Christmas and New Year period when drinking habits would certainly have been highly atypical. The first author, sometimes alone, sometimes accompanied by as many as three colleagues, visited each of the five schools and administered the initial self-completed questionnaires to groups of pupils ranging from 20 to 200 during school hours. Head teachers and their staff ensured that all potential respondents were given copies of the duplicated letter to parents outlining the aims and methods of the study and providing an opportunity for them to withdraw their children from participation in fieldwork. The self-completed questionnaire covered the following topics: biographical details, parental drinking status and parental attitudes to respondent's use of alcohol, recollection of alcohol education in school or elsewhere, self-reported drinking habits, experiences related to drinking (including alcohol-related consequences), and attitudes to the use and misuse of alcohol.

Respondents were asked to supply in full their names and home addresses. Two additional names and addresses, such as those of a close friend or a relative, were also requested from each respondent to facilitate follow-up during the third phase of the study. It was emphasized that while these addresses were requested, individuals would be free to refuse to co-operate with the follow-up if and when they were eventually sought for reinterview.

RESULTS

Response

A total of 1,036 students completed questionnaires. Only four students refused to co-operate with the study or were restrained by their parents from doing so. This constituted a net response rate of 99.6 per cent. Refusal was the only reason for non-response. An average of four visits to each school enabled the first author and his associates to contact all 1,040 potential respondents. The pattern of response is shown in *Table 4*. Some respondents failed to answer some of the questions contained in the self-completed instrument. In consequence, the totals presented in this chapter vary from item to item.

Table 4 Pattern of response to the initial phase of the study

school	respondents		refusals	total
	males	females		
1	117	154	—	271
2	78	97	1 female	176
3	121	126	1 male	248
4	120	103	1 male	224
5	48	72	1 female	121
total	484	552	4	1,040

(School 5 was the private school.)

Biographical Characteristics

A total of 46.7 per cent of the study group were male, 90.9 per cent were Scots born, and 83.9 per cent were currently living with both parents. In addition, 55.6 per cent reported that their fathers were manual workers. These biographical characteristics are summarized in *Table 5*.

The occupational background of the study group was virtually indistinguishable from that of the overall population of the Lothian Region. The 1981 sample Census showed that 45.6 per cent of residents in the region lived in households headed by a non-manual worker (Registrar General Scotland 1982: I, 13). A slightly different picture of the 'representativeness' of the study group was obtained from the third, more detailed, wave of data collection. This is described in the next chapter.

Table 5 Biographical characteristics of the study group

	n	%★
SEX		
males	484	46.7
females	552	53.3
total	1,036	100.0
BIRTHPLACE		
Scotland	942	90.9
elsewhere in UK	74	7.1
outside UK	20	1.9
total	1,036	99.9
OCCUPATION OF FATHER/STEPFATHER		
manual	527	55.6
non-manual	421	44.4
total	948	100.0
LIVING WITH PARENTS OR GUARDIANS		
both parents	868	83.9
mother and stepfather	40	3.9
father and stepmother	6	0.6
mother only	89	8.6
father only	18	1.7
grandparents	2	0.2
other guardians	9	0.9
none of these	3	0.3
total	1,035	100.1

★calculated to nearest decimal point

Self-reported Alcohol Consumption

Only 2 per cent of both male and female respondents reported never having tasted an alcoholic drink. The average age at which male respondents reported having tried their first drink was significantly lower than that reported by females, 10.3 years compared with 11.6 years. (Throughout this book the word 'significant' is used to refer to real differences or associations indicated by statistical tests. This means that results could only have occurred by chance in 5 per cent, 1 per cent, or 0.1 per cent of samples.)

As shown by *Table 6*, just over half of the males, 50.2 per cent,

Table 6 Age of first alcoholic drink

age	males		females	
	n	%	n	%
6 or under	58	12.4	31	5.8
7–8	69	14.8	29	5.4
9–10	107	23.0	92	17.2
11–12	117	25.1	156	29.2
13–14	101	21.7	185	34.6
15 or older	14	3.0	42	7.8
total	466	100.0	535	100.0

reported having tried their first alcoholic drink before the age of 10, compared with only 28.4 per cent of the females.

There were no significant differences between male and female respondents' accounts of who had given them their first alcoholic drink. The majority, 65.9 per cent of males and 62.1 per cent of females, reported that they had been given their first drink by their parents, stepparents or other guardians.

Table 7 Who gave respondents their first taste of alcohol

initiator	males		females	
	n	%*	n	%
parent/stepparent/guardian	289	62.1	350	65.9
sibling	35	7.5	25	4.7
an adult other than parent, stepparent, or guardian	51	10.9	66	12.4
boy or girl of the same age	48	10.3	54	10.2
other people	42	9.1	36	6.8
total	465	99.9	531	100.0

*calculated to nearest decimal point

As shown in *Table 7*, the great majority of respondents had been introduced to alcohol by close family members. Only 10 per cent of both males and females reported having been introduced to alcohol by non-siblings of their own age and fewer still reported having been given their first drink by adults other than parents, stepparents, or other guardians.

Respondents were far more likely to report having last consumed

Table 8 Location of most recent drink

location	males		females	
	n	%*	*n*	%
in own home	180	38.5	188	35.7
in home of adult relative or friends of parents	43	9.2	68	12.9
in home of friend	51	10.9	59	11.2
in public house or hotel	80	17.1	102	19.3
in open air (street, park, etc.)	34	7.3	61	11.6
at dance	51	10.9	26	4.9
elsewhere	28	6.0	23	4.4
total	467	99.9	527	100.0

*calculated to nearest decimal point

alcohol in their own homes than elsewhere. As shown in *Table 8*, there was a significant difference between the location of last drinking reported by respondents of either sex.

There was no significant difference between the proportions of males and females reporting that their last drink was in their own home, or in the home of others, or in public bars. Even so, males were significantly more likely than females to report having consumed their last drink at a dance; 51 out of 467, compared with only 26 out of 527. Conversely, females were significantly more likely than males to report having consumed their last drink in the open air; 61 out of 527 compared with only 34 out of 467.

Table 9 Recency of last drink (drinkers only)

recentness	males		females	
	n	%	*n*	%
within past week	208	45.2	166	31.7
1–2 weeks ago	76	16.5	104	19.9
3–4 weeks ago	51	11.1	62	11.8
over 4 weeks–3 months ago	44	9.6	74	14.1
over 3 months ago	81	17.6	118	22.5
total	460	100.0	524	100.0

Respondents were asked when they last had a drink. As *Table 9* shows, 45.2 per cent of the males and 31.7 per cent of the females who answered this question reported having consumed alcohol during the previous week. As *Table 9* shows, males were significantly more likely than females to report having had a drink either during the previous week or recently.

Previous Week's Drinking

In fact, 263 (54.3 per cent) of the males and 237 (42.9 per cent) of the females supplied details of their alcohol consumption during the week preceding data collection. The disparity between these responses and those related to recency of alcohol consumption suggests that the earlier question: 'When did you last have a drink?', may have been answered inaccurately by some respondents who, upon more careful consideration, then supplied details of drinks they had consumed during the previous week. An alternative possibility is that some respondents who had not consumed alcohol in the past week in fact supplied details of either their most recent or a typical week's consumption. It must be emphasized that the relevant question was phrased to avoid such mistakes: 'Think carefully over the last seven days. Please write in exactly what alcoholic drinks you have consumed on each day during the past week. For each day write in: the number of pints of beer etc. . . . that you have drunk. Try to remember where you were and who you were with on each day. This may help you remember what you have had to drink.'

Previous week's alcohol consumption data were recorded in units of alcohol. Each unit is equivalent to either a single glass (half-pint) of beer, lager, stout, cider, etc., or to a single measure of spirits or wine. Each of these units contains *roughly* 1.0 centilitre or 7.9 grammes of absolute alcohol. (The normal Scottish measure of spirits is one-fifth of a gill. Some lager contains 2.2 centilitres in half a pint, while some beers contain only 1.0 centilitre. There is no standard measure for a glass of wine.)

The average levels of previous week's consumption per drinker were 17.8 units for males and 9.2 units for females. The overall distribution of previous week's self-reported alcohol consumption is shown in *Table 10*.

Consistent with their much higher level of alcohol consumption, male respondents who reported drinking during the previous week stated that they had drunk alcohol on significantly more days than had

Table 10 Previous week's self-reported alcohol consumption (drinkers only)

units consumed	males		females	
	n	%*	n	%
1–2	57	21.7	92	38.8
3–4	40	15.2	42	17.7
5–6	28	10.6	26	11.0
7–8	18	6.8	8	3.4
9–10	9	3.4	16	6.7
11–15	26	9.9	24	10.1
16–20	25	9.5	12	5.1
21–30	21	8.0	7	3.0
31–50	18	6.8	6	2.5
51–100	19	7.2	0	0.0
101 or more	2	0.7	4	1.7
total	263	99.8	237	100.0

*calculated to the nearest decimal point

their female counterparts: 2.3 days compared with only 1.9 days. The average maximum daily consumption reported by males during the previous week was significantly higher than that reported by females: 9.1 units compared with only 4.8 units. These results show that, on average, respondents who reported previous week's alcohol consumption had consumed over half of their total week's intake in a single day. This was the case for 53 per cent of males and 52 per cent of females.

A General Measure of Alcohol Consumption

While 98 per cent of the study group reported having tasted alcohol, only 45.2 per cent of males and 31.7 per cent of females reported having done so during the week preceding data collection. As noted above, confusingly, 54.3 per cent of the males and 42.9 per cent of the females also supplied a detailed account of their previous (or in some cases the most recent) week's alcohol consumption. It had been anticipated, and piloting had confirmed, that many 15–16-year-old students would in fact not have drunk during the previous week. *Table 9* confirms this. Accordingly, an alternative, more widely appropriate, measure of self-reported alcohol consumption is examined. This relates to the last drinking occasion regardless of whether or not it occurred during the week preceding data collection.

Altogether, 95.5 per cent of male respondents and 92.9 per cent of the females provided details of the amounts of alcohol they consumed on their last drinking occasion. Since an additional 2 per cent of respondents of either sex had declared that they had never tasted alcohol, this meant that only 2.5 per cent of eligible males and 4.9 per cent of females did not supply data related to their last drinking

Table 11 Alcohol consumption on last drinking occasion

units	males		females	
	n	%*	n	%
1–2	155	33.5	190	37.0
3–4	95	20.6	127	24.8
5–6	68	14.7	84	16.4
7–8	46	9.9	41	8.0
9–10	29	6.3	20	3.9
11–12	23	5.0	21	4.1
13–14	11	2.4	13	2.5
15–16	6	1.3	7	1.4
17–18	7	1.5	5	1.0
19–20	7	1.5	2	0.4
21 or more	15	3.2	3	0.6
total	462	99.9	513	100.1

*calculated to nearest decimal point

occasion. The reasons for this non-response are unclear but can probably be attributed to accidental omission, poor recollection, or to undeclared non-drinkers. Even so, details of the last drinking occasion were provided by the overwhelming majority of those who reported ever having tasted alcohol. This information is used throughout this chapter as the primary general measure of self-reported alcohol consumption.

The average consumption reported by male respondents on their last drinking occasion was significantly, though not greatly, higher than the equivalent reported by the females; 5.3 units compared with 4.1 units.

The distribution of consumption during the last drinking occasion is shown in *Table 11*.

The difference between the average levels of consumption reported by the sexes was not nearly as great as those discrepancies noted above in relation to previous week's drinking. This is illustrated by *Table 12*.

As *Table 12* shows, the average consumption of males on their last drinking occasion was only 29.3 per cent higher than the corresponding level reported by females. This difference is only half that existing

Table 12 Sex differences in average measures of alcohol consumption

measures (units)	males	females (units)	% difference
weekly total*	17.8	9.2	93.3
maximum daily*	9.1	4.8	89.6
drinking day*	7.7	4.8	60.4
last occasion**	5.3	4.1	29.3

*measures relate to drinking during week before data collection (n = 500)
**general measure of alcohol consumption (n = 975)

between the sexes in relation to the average drinking day reported during the week preceding data collection. This disparity is rather perplexing. However, alcohol consumption levels reported by those who had not had a drink during the previous week were 24 per cent lower than those who had consumed alcohol within the past seven days. A partial explanation of this disparity may therefore be that less recent consumption was not so well remembered or so accurately described as recent drinking. Overall the recency of last drink was significantly negatively correlated with the amount reportedly consumed on that occasion. This has been noted in other studies, for example by Wilson (1980a).

From a comparison of data provided by respondents who described both their last drinking occasion and their drinking during the previous week, it emerged that these two measures were significantly positively correlated. It is of interest that the various average levels of daily alcohol consumption reported by females and shown in *Table 12* were remarkably constant. These differed by only 17 per cent, while those of the

Table 13 Experience of the consequences of drinking (males and females)

type of consequence	males		females		significance
	n	%[1]	n	%[2]	
a) DRUNKENNESS					
i) have ever been 'merry', 'a little bit drunk', or 'very drunk'	331	70.4	327	61.0	*
ii) having been 'merry' in past 6 months	296	62.9	310	57.8	NS
iii) having been 'a little bit drunk' in past 6 months	236	50.2	233	43.5	*
iv) having been 'very drunk' in past 6 months	171	36.4	128	23.9	*
v) experience of hangover (ever)	144	30.6	141	26.3	NS
vi) having had a hangover in past 6 months	120	25.5	121	22.6	NS
vii) have had drink in morning to steady nerves or get rid of hangover	26	5.5	16	3.0	NS
b) HEALTH					
i) have been advised by doctor to drink less	10	2.1	7	1.3	NS
ii) have had alcohol-related accident/injury	42	8.9	27	5.1	*
iii) have had 'upset stomach' due to drinking	189	40.2	155	28.9	*
iv) have had stomach ulcer	4	0.8	—	—	—
v) have had 'liver trouble'	2	0.4	3	0.6	NS
vi) have had shaky hand in morning after drinking	26	5.5	30	5.6	NS

c) SOCIAL

i) have disagreed with parents because of drink	87	18.5	108	20.1	NS
ii) have had own drinking criticized	81	17.2	60	11.2	*
iii) have experienced school problems due to drinking	9	1.9	12	2.2	NS
iv) have spent too much money on drinking	124	26.4	76	14.2	*
v) have quarrelled due to own drinking	53	11.3	45	8.4	NS
vi) have had financial problems due to own drinking	46	9.8	15	2.8	*
vii) have arrived late at school due to drinking	11	2.3	12	2.2	NS
viii) have missed a day's schooling due to drinking	16	3.4	11	2.1	NS

d) SELF-ASCRIPTION

i) have been worried about own drinking	27	5.7	19	3.5	NS
ii) have experienced alcohol-related problems	37	7.9	24	4.4	*

NS = not significant
*significant difference
[1] calculated in relation to the 470 males who reported having at some time tasted alcohol
[2] calculated in relation to the 536 females who reported having at some time tasted alcohol

males differed by 72 per cent. These results show that while, in general, recent drinkers were heavier drinkers, this difference was markedly greater amongst the males who exhibited a much greater variation in alcohol consumption levels than females in relation to their recency (and presumably regularity) of drinking.

Self-reporting of alcohol consumption on the last drinking occasion may have been distorted by poorer recollection of more distant events. This measure is nevertheless adopted as the most useful indicator of consumption since it applies to a far higher proportion of the study group than do data related to previous week's drinking. Accordingly, whenever 'alcohol consumption' is mentioned in this chapter, it refers to the last drinking occasion.

The Consequences of Drinking

Data were obtained relating to twenty-three questions concerned with some of the possible consequences of drinking. Twenty-one of these items, such as experience of a hangover, were by definition alcohol-related. The remaining items were experience of a stomach ulcer and 'liver trouble'. While it is extensively documented that both of these conditions are generally associated with alcohol misuse, neither is solely alcohol-related and, particularly in relation to this very young group of respondents, it is conceded that the occurrence of either condition was in fact probably not attributable to excessive drinking. The levels of reported experience of these consequences are shown in *Table 13*.

As *Table 13* indicates, the general level of consequences reportedly experienced by male respondents was higher than that reported by females. Even so, significant differences between the sexes existed in relation to only nine of the twenty-three items. These were general experience of some degree of intoxication, experience of being both 'a little bit drunk' or 'very drunk' during the past six months, experience of an alcohol-related accident or injury, upset stomach, criticism of own drinking, having spent too much money on drinking, experience of financial problems, or admission of having experienced alcohol-related problems. As expected, some of the health items such as those relating to stomach ulcers and liver trouble were reported by very few respondents of either sex. It is not unexpected that males, generally heavier drinkers than females, reported significantly higher levels of experience in relation to some items. What is perhaps more interesting is that in relation to the remaining items there was no significant difference between the sexes. These were (excluding stomach ulcers and liver trouble): experience of 'being merry' during the past six months (reported by 60.2 per cent of drinkers), recent experience of hangovers, having had a drink the morning after drinking, having disagreed with parents about drinking, having experienced school problems due to drinking, having quarrelled, having arrived late at school, or missed a day's schooling due to drinking, or having been worried about own drinking. It is clear from these data that while males remained more likely than females to experience some of the possible consequences of (heavy) drinking, such sequelae were by no means a male monopoly. The average male who had tasted alcohol reported having experienced a mean of 5.1 of the twenty-three consequences compared with 4.2 experienced by his female counterpart. As one would expect, the total number of consequences reportedly experienced by respondents was significantly positively correlated with their alcohol consumption.

As *Table 13* illustrates, virtually all of the twenty-three individual consequences were significantly positively correlated with alcohol consumption. The exceptions were: having been advised by a doctor to drink less (significant for females only), having had stomach ulcers or liver trouble (significant for neither sex), and admission of having experienced alcohol-related problems at school (significant for females only). *Figure 2* shows how average consequences scores varied at different levels of alcohol consumption for each sex. It must be emphasized that a consequences score of five might only have implied having been 'merry', a 'little bit drunk', or 'very drunk', or 'ever' having had a hangover. These items are clearly neither discrete nor particularly serious.

Figure 2 shows that the average number of consequences reportedly experienced by both sexes at specific levels of alcohol consumption was similar. The degree of similarity in relation to consequences associated with specific alcohol consumption levels may be partly illustrated in relation to the heaviest drinking 5 per cent of either sex who supplied details of their last drinking occasion. Amongst these individuals, twenty-three males and twenty-six females, average consequences scores were not significantly different, 8.8 and 8.6 respectively. In addition, the males had consumed only 21 per cent more than the females, 19 units compared with 15 units. Referring further to *Figure 2*, it is of interest to note that for both sexes the 'threshold' level of alcohol consumption beyond which average consequences scores exceeded 6 (as noted above, lower scores may mean little) was 6 to 8 units. There are some anomalies in *Figure 2*. These relate to curiously low consequences scores amongst heavy drinkers. Such discrepancies involve extremely few respondents and are probably attributable to the rate of instability generated by such small numbers.

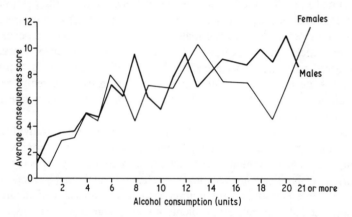

Figure 2. Average levels of consequences at different levels of alcohol consumption

The Extent of the Consequences of Drinking

Only 20.2 per cent of the study group reported not having experienced at least one of the list of twenty-three possible consequences of drinking. As noted above, 2 per cent of respondents had never tasted alcohol, so only 18.2 per cent of those who had done so had not experienced any of the alcohol-related consequences. The general extent of these consequences is shown in *Table 14*.

As mentioned above, some of the twenty-three consequences examined were neither particularly serious, nor were they necessarily discrete. Even so, as *Table 14* shows, 39.5 per cent of males and 31.3 per cent of female respondents reported having experienced six or more consequences.

Table 14 The extent of the consequences of drinking*

number of	males		females	
consequences	*n*	%**	*n*	%**
0	76	15.7	133	24.1
1	22	4.5	24	4.3
2	31	6.4	25	4.5
3	38	7.9	50	9.0
4	66	13.6	91	16.5
5	60	12.4	56	10.1
6	47	9.7	49	8.9
7	36	7.4	40	7.2
8	31	6.4	27	4.9
9	24	5.0	22	4.0
10	21	4.3	10	1.8
11	10	2.1	12	2.2
12	7	1.4	3	0.5
13	8	1.6	6	1.1
14	1	0.2	3	0.5
15	3	0.6	0	—
16	1	0.2	0	—
17	1	0.2	1	0.2
18	1	0.2	0	—
total	484	99.8	552	99.8

*this table relates to the entire study group (n = 1,036)
**calculated to nearest decimal point

The Correlates of Six Serious Consequences

Six alcohol-related consequences were selected which the authors considered to be 'serious'. These were: having had four or more hangovers in the previous six months; having had a drink in the morning to steady nerves or get rid of hangover; having been advised by a doctor to drink less; having had an alcohol-related accident or injury; having a shaky hand in the morning after drinking; and having missed a day at school due to drinking.

Experience of one or more of these serious consequences was admitted by 166 respondents, 95 males and 71 females (20.2 per cent and 13.2 per cent respectively of those who had tasted alcohol). This difference between the sexes was statistically significant.

Table 15 The extent of serious alcohol-related consequences

number of serious consequences experienced	males		females	
	n	%	n	%
1	71	15.1	51	9.5
2	14	3.0	14	2.6
3	7	1.5	4	0.7
4	1	0.2	1	0.2
5	—	—	1	0.2
6	2	0.4	—	—
totals	95	20.2	71	13.2

Illicit Drug Use

Respondents were asked whether or not they had ever tried any of the following drugs either out of curiosity or 'for kicks': cannabis, LSD, barbiturates, Mogadon, Librium, Valium, glues or solvents, amphetamines, opium, morphine, heroin, cocaine, tranquillizers, or other drugs.

Altogether, 15.2 per cent of males and 10.7 per cent of females reported having at some time tried at least one type of drug. Some respondents had used more than one drug; 4.5 per cent of males and 3.6 per cent of females. The extent of the self-reported use of specific drugs is shown in *Table 16*.

Self-reported illicit drug use was unrelated to social class, school, country of birth, or to whether or not respondents were living with their natural parents. Even so, drug use was significantly positively correlated with alcohol consumption levels, tobacco consumption, and the number of serious alcohol-related consequences experienced.

The 133 respondents who had used one or more drugs were examined separately. The relationship was investigated between the number of drugs used and alcohol-related consequences experienced. This analysis revealed that the extent of drug use was significantly positively correlated both with the overall number of consequences reported and with the number of serious consequences reported.

Recollection of Alcohol Education

Respondents were asked whether or not they had received alcohol education or had been shown a film about alcohol while in school.

Almost exactly half, 49.9 per cent of the study group, reported having had alcohol education and 27.5 per cent reported having seen a film about alcohol. The level of recalled exposure to alcohol education ranged from 20.2 per cent in one school to 92.8 per cent in a second, while the level of recalled exposure to films about alcohol ranged from only 4.6 per cent to 91.5 per cent.

Table 16 Self-reported levels of illicit drug use

drug	males	females	total
	%	%	%
cannabis	7.4	7.1	7.2
LSD	1.2	1.1	1.2
barbiturates	1.4	1.3	1.4
Mogadon	1.4	0.5	1.0
Librium (chlordiazepoxide hydrochloride)	0.4	0.4	0.4
Valium (diazepam)	4.5	3.8	4.2
glues and solvents	5.4	4.0	4.6
amphetamines	1.9	3.1	2.5
opium	0.8	0.5	0.7
morphine	0.4	0.2	0.3
heroin	1.0	0.4	1.0
cocaine	1.7	0.4	1.0
tranquillizers	5.4	5.1	5.2
other drugs	4.3	3.8	4.1

(74 males and 59 females reported having used one or more types of illicit drug)

An independent assessment of the likely level of exposure to alcohol education amongst respondents within each of the five schools was obtained. This information was provided either by head teachers or in some cases by another member of the teaching staff. This revealed that in three of the five schools pupils provided evidence of a far lower level of experience of alcohol education than was anticipated by the independent view. In the case of one school, respondents also reported a much lower level of recollection of a film about alcohol than was indicated independently. The patterns of exposure reported by students and by staff are shown in *Table 17*.

As shown by *Table 17*, only in one of the five schools did the level of alcohol education reported by students fall within the range estimated by staff.

Three of the five co-operating schools were reported by members of teaching staff to have a policy of ensuring that all pupils received some education or information about alcohol. A member of staff from one of the two schools without such a policy provided the following explanation: 'Our approach to this form of education is "light". It has been found that too intensive a course in topics of this nature tends to have an effect which is the opposite of that desired.'

Staff comments from two of the three schools which sought to provide all pupils with alcohol education were extremely pessimistic:

School A: 'It seems to me with all the present efforts in alcohol education, we are being singularly unsuccessful. Pupils' attitudes seem already crystallized by the time they are in secondary school; possibly formed by the examples they have seen of parents, etc. . . . '

School B: 'We eventually found that talks on alcohol and the dangers of alcoholism, especially to older pupils, were greeted with a certain weariness. When the pupils were asked about this they said that they had heard it often before.'

Table 17 Recollection of alcohol education and films about alcohol

school	alcohol education		films about alcohol	
	students' replies	staff estimate	students' replies	staff estimate
	%	%	%	%
1	39.1	50–74	7.7	1–24
2	40.6	75 or more	4.6	1–24
3	20.2	75 or more	16.6	75 or more
4	92.8	50–74	91.5	1–24
5	68.3	50–74	6.7	1–24

ALCOHOL EDUCATION AND ATTITUDES TO ALCOHOL

From the preceding statements it is clear that alcohol education was not generally viewed with enthusiasm or optimism by teachers from the five co-operating schools. Substantial sections of the self-completed questionnaire were concerned with alcohol education and attitudes to drinking and alcohol. Space does not permit a detailed description of these items or a lengthy discussion of their interrelationships or association with other variables. Even so, it is important to note that neither reported experience of varying amounts and types of alcohol education, nor attitudes to drinking and alcohol, was found to be significantly associated, either with alcohol consumption or with any of the twenty-three consequences associated with it.

Comparison With Other Studies

Several studies of teenage alcohol use have previously been carried out in Britain and Ireland (Davies and Stacey 1972; O'Connor 1978; Hawker 1978). In addition, two recent surveys have produced information about self-reported drinking habits amongst the general population in Scotland (Dight 1976) and in England and Wales (Wilson 1980a). The latter study, together with that carried out by Hawker, also collected data relating to some of the possible consequences of drinking broadly similar to those obtained by the initial phase of the present study. Additional Scottish information about drinking habits has been produced by Plant and Pirie (1979), Saunders and Kershaw (1978), Plant (1979a), and Davies (1980). These studies permit a few points of comparison with the present exercise to be made. Even so, comparability is extremely restricted since samples and methods may vary considerably between different studies.

General Level of Drinking

In the present study, 98 per cent of both males and females reported having tasted alcohol. This result is identical to that related to 15- and 16-year-olds obtained by Hawker's 1975–76 survey of adolescents in various areas of England. The earlier Glasgow study of teenagers by Davies and Stacey had produced slightly different results. These showed that amongst boys, 94.7 per cent had tasted alcohol at the age of 15, and that this rose to only 96.6 per cent one year later. Amongst girls, 93.7 per cent and 95.3 per cent reported having tasted alcohol at the ages of 15 and 16 respectively. While these levels of experience are not very different from those noted in the present study, they are consistent with more general evidence that during the 1960s and 1970s levels of alcohol consumption in Britain increased considerably and that the percentage of non-drinkers in the population has been declining (Plant

1982). The differences between the Glasgow study and the present investigation are trivial and to a large extent may be because these studies were carried out at different times and in different areas. It is notable that the general level of alcohol use and misuse in this and other British studies is markedly higher than that noted by comparable studies in the United States. Rachel *et al.* (1980) noted that only about 80 per cent of American adolescents aged 16 and over had consumed alcoholic beverages.

Age of First Drink

Both in the present study and that by Davies and Stacey, the common age of first drinking reported by teenage respondents was 13–14. In Hawker's English study it was 13 years. All three studies indicated that girls had a slightly, but not significantly, later introduction to drinking than did their male counterparts.

Initiators

In the present study, 62.1 per cent of males and 65.9 per cent of females reported having been given their first drink by their parents, step-parents or guardians. Hawker found that 54 per cent of both males and females reported having been introduced to alcohol by a parent. Davies and Stacey found that parents played a less important role. In their study, only 47.4 per cent of males and 39.6 per cent of females stated that they had been given their first drink by their parents. These differences are probably partly due to different methods of the three studies. They are, however, also consistent with the recent trend for alcohol to be increasingly kept and consumed at home.

Previous Week's Drinking

The studies by Davies and Stacey, Hawker, and O'Connor did not collect comparable alcohol consumption data to those obtained in the present exercise. Indeed, the feasibility of obtaining such data from teenagers has been seriously disputed. Hawker, for example, concluded that such a quest was unjustified:

'After the pilot study was completed, it was decided not to try to analyse the actual amount of alcohol consumed either as an average or on any one particular occasion. It was quite obvious that asking children to report on actual amounts of alcohol has severe drawbacks. In many cases they were ignorant of standard measures and

---

tended to drink from a variety of glasses and bottles. An accurate estimate of actual alcohol consumed would, therefore, be impossible.'

(Hawker 1978: 25)

Some comparative data are available from other sources. Dight's *Survey of Scottish Drinking Habits* (Dight 1976) elicited some broadly similar data, as did Plant and Pirie (1979) in a survey of four Scottish towns, and Wilson (1980a) in relation to England and Wales. Each of these three surveys is of only limited relevance, since all three were based upon general population samples of people aged 17 (or in Wilson's study 18 and above) drawn from the Electoral Register.

Table 18 shows how the results of the present study related to those obtained by Dight and by Wilson.

In the present study, 45.2 per cent of males and 31.7 per cent of females reported having consumed alcohol during the previous week. As one would expect, these percentages are lower than those produced

Table 18 Comparison of previous week's alcohol consumption data with studies by Dight and by Wilson

	present study	Dight	Wilson
date of fieldwork	1979–80	1972	1978
coverage	Lothian Region	Scotland	England and Wales
age of subjects	15–16	17 and over	18 and over
percentage of males who were 'regular drinkers'	45.2	74.0	76.0
percentage of females who were 'regular drinkers'	31.7	46.0	58.0
per capita consumption of male regular drinkers	17.8 units	26.2 units★ (+47.2%)★★	32.2★★★ (+80.9%)★★
per capita consumption of female regular drinkers	9.2 units	5.6 units★ (−64.3%)★★	13.7★★★ (+40.2%)★★

★figures relate to respondents aged 17–21
★★figures in brackets indicate percentage difference from present study; + = more than present study; − = less than present study
★★★figures related to respondents aged 18–24. These figures are approximate

for the general (and older) population by Dight, 74 per cent and 46 per cent respectively. Wilson's more recent population survey of England and Wales showed that 76 per cent of males and 58 per cent of females had consumed alcohol during the previous week.

In the present study, the average amounts reportedly consumed by those who had drunk alcohol in the previous week were 17.8 units for males and 9.2 units for females. Predictably these quantities are generally lower than those reported by rather older respondents in other studies. In Dight's survey the amounts reportedly consumed by 'regular drinkers' (those having drunk during the previous week) aged 17–21 years were 26.2 units for males and 5.6 units for females. Male 'regular drinkers' in the present study had consumed 47 per cent less than their near counterparts in Dight's study. The discrepancy between the females in the present study and those noted by Dight was interesting. Dight's 17–21-year-olds had drunk 64 per cent less than those aged 15–16 in this investigation. In Wilson's more recent survey in England and Wales, higher average levels of consumption were reported by 'regular drinkers', especially by females. Males aged 18–24 years reported an average consumption of approximately 32.2 units, while females reported drinking an average of approximately 13.7 units.

A more recent survey of drinking habits in Scotland was carried out in 1978 by Wilson (1980b). This, together with a parallel exercise in Northern Ireland and the study of England and Wales referred to above, permits a further source of comparative data for the present study.

The most salient conclusion from these 1978 national surveys was that patterns of alcohol consumption amongst men in Scotland were strikingly similar to those in England and Wales. Male 'regular drinkers' in Scotland, aged 20–7, had an average previous week's per capita consumption of 26.2 units, while those in England and Wales consumed slightly but not significantly more, 26.6 units. In Northern Ireland the corresponding figure was lower, 18.9 units. Amongst females aged 20–7 there was similarly not a great difference between Scottish data and those relating to England and Wales. The previous week's per capita consumption reported by young Scottish female 'regular drinkers' was 7.7 units, while that reported by their English and Welsh counterparts was, like the results for males, insignificantly higher, 9.7 units. Young women in Northern Ireland had a per capita consumption of 7.0 units. These 1978 data certainly give a much more recent general picture of alcohol consumption than does the 1972 study by Dight. Between Dight's survey and the initial phase of the present investigation that was conducted in 1979 and 1980, alcohol consumption in the United Kingdom increased substantially. Per capita beer consumption rose by 13 per cent, while that of wines and spirits increased by 72.1 per cent and 84.4 per cent respectively (Brewers' Society 1982). The big increases in wines and spirits are particularly relevant to females (Shaw 1980). Wilson (1980b) casts doubt upon the suggestion that Scottish alcohol consumption changed much between 1972 and 1978:

'In fact, the amounts consumed in Scotland have changed little between 1972 (when an earlier O.P.C.S. survey was carried out) and 1978. Although comparable results are not available for England and Wales, the 29 per cent increase between 1972 and 1978 in the total United Kingdom consumption (from Customs and Excise figures) implies an increase of that order in the amounts consumed in England and Wales. Thus consumption levels in Scotland in 1972 would have been considerably higher than the levels in England and Wales.'

(Wilson 1980a: 15)

The Consequences of Drinking

As noted above, exactly comparable data to those collected by the present study are sparse. Even so, the surveys by Hawker and Wilson (1980a) did obtain information relating to some of the same consequences as those examined in the present study. The similarities between the reported prevalence of these consequences are shown in *Table 19*.

The data presented in *Table 19* must be set in the context of fairly major limitations. The study by Hawker related to subjects aged 13–16, while that by Wilson related to people aged 18 and over. The studies were carried out in England (Hawker) and England and Wales (Wilson). The present study collected data related to consequences experienced either within the previous six months or at any time. Hawker collected consequences data relating to the previous year while Wilson had yet another time span, the previous three months. It is therefore surprising that less than 10 per cent difference in reported levels of consequences was reported in relation to the following items:

(a) Percentage having been drunk at least once: Hawker (both sexes); Wilson (males only)

(b) Percentage experiencing a hangover at least once: Hawker (both sexes)

(c) Percentage having had their drinking criticized: Wilson (males only)

(d) Percentage having missed a day's school due to drinking: Hawker (both sexes).

With further reference to *Table 19*, it is evident that in absolute terms data relating to having a shaky hand in the morning after drinking were very similar in Wilson's survey to those collected by the present study.

Validity

Self-reported alcohol consumption data are widely believed to be subject to considerable misreporting, particularly by individuals who are in fact heavy drinkers or who have experienced alcohol-related problems. The imperfections of such data have been reviewed elsewhere (Kreitman 1977; Plant 1979a). As noted above, Hawker (1978) has asserted that it is not feasible to collect accurate details of alcohol consumption from teenagers. The present authors do not share this view. It is conceded that many teenagers probably do give rather imprecise information concerning their alcohol intake. The evidence of this study did not indicate that teenagers were any less likely than other respondents to provide accurate details of their alcohol consumption. Pre-testing, piloting, and the first two waves of data collection showed that the young respondents were overwhelmingly able to supply alcohol consumption data without undue difficulty, although a minority asked for clarification concerning the classification of some of the more exotic beverages which they had imbibed. Only a tiny number of responses obtained were obviously suspect. One male respondent, for example, claimed to have consumed the equivalent of 23 pints of beer or nearly one and a half bottles of spirits during his last drinking occasion. This is unlikely. Such very few suspicious responses made no statistical impact upon the general conclusions of this study. The authors conclude, consistent with observations by Wilson, that most of the respondents provided plausible and probably reasonably truthful responses both in relation to alcohol consumption and to other items including the possibly more sensitive topics related to the consequences of drinking.

Table 19 Comparison of levels of consequences with studies by Hawker and by Wilson

consequence	present study	Hawker		Wilson	
percentage having been drunk at least once					
males	63.0*	68.0**	(+7.9%)***	57.0****	(−10.5%)***
females	58.0*	66.0**	(+13.8%)	32.0****	(−81.2%)***
percentage experiencing a hangover at least once					
males	25.0*	25.0**	(0.0%)*	—	
females	23.0*	24.0**	(+4.3%)	—	
percentage having had a drink in the morning to steady nerves or get rid of hangover					
males	5.0*****	—		4.0****	(−25.0%)***
females	3.0*****	—		2.0****	(−50.0%)***
percentage having had shaky hand in morning after drinking					
males	5.0*****	—		3.0****	(−66.6%)***
females	6.0*****	—		4.0****	(−50.0%)***
percentage having had their drinking criticized					
males	17.0*****	—		18.0****	(+5.9%)***
females	11.0*****	—		4.0****	(−175.0%)***
percentage having missed a day's school due to drinking					
males	3.0*****	3.0**	(0.0%)	—	
females	2.0*****	2.0**	(0.0%)	—	

*refers to past six months
**refers to past year
***figures in brackets indicate percentage difference from present study; + = more than present study; − = less than present study
****refers to past three months
*****refers to experience at any time

In addition, fieldwork revealed (again in contrast to Hawker) that it was possible to classify the paternal occupation of the great majority of respondents, though only by a very simple manual/non-manual dichotomy. This was achieved by verbal explanations by the first author and individual guidance to a substantial minority of the study group, while completing the questionnaire. Further support for the validity of the alcohol consumption data reported in this chapter is derived from the consistency of these data with other items, notably those related to the consequences of drinking. It is therefore concluded that while these data should not be treated as a precise measure of reality, as in other self-reported alcohol consumption surveys, they probably do give an acceptable impression of the drinking habits of most of the study group.

DISCUSSION

The results of this initial phase indicate that a substantial minority of the study group were drinking regularly and that the mean level of alcohol consumption of these 'regular drinkers' (retaining Susan Dight's definition) was high, and particularly so amongst females. The most striking feature of the data presented in *Table 18* is that female 'regular drinkers' in the present study had a mean consumption 64.3 per cent *higher* than that obtained from Dight's respondents aged 17 to 21 in 1972. This remarkable disparity is consistent with more general evidence that levels of alcohol consumption have risen disproportionately amongst young women during the past decade (Plant 1981a; Shaw 1980). These results lend support to the view that the difference between the drinking habits of the sexes is diminishing. The smoking habits reported by the study group were equally striking since, while 30 per cent of the males reported being smokers, 37 per cent of the females also did so. These results are broadly, though not completely, in line with those of two recent surveys of smoking amongst Scottish teenagers. The first of these was a study carried out by Ledwith during 1981 (Ledwith 1983). This was also conducted in the Lothian Region and collected data from school students aged 11–16. Like the present study, this concluded that amongst 15- and 16-year-olds, females were more likely to smoke than were males. Ledwith's study concluded that 38 per cent of girls and 23 per cent of boys aged 15 and 16 respectively smoke. These results were almost identical to the 37 per cent noted in the present study. Even so, Ledwith obtained rather lower levels of smoking, 24 per cent and 23 per cent respectively amongst males aged 15 and 16. The present study obtained a figure of 30 per cent.

A survey of 574 Scottish school pupils aged 15–16 was conducted during 1982 by Dobbs and Marsh (1983). This concluded that 34 per cent of boys and 33 per cent of females were smokers. Ledwith's Lothian data are more directly comparable to the present study, since they were obtained from the same area and only about one year later. The survey by Dobbs and Marsh was a national exercise covering England, Wales, and Scotland. This indicated that the pattern of smoking amongst secondary-school pupils in Scotland was very similar to that amongst their counterparts elsewhere in Britain.

The present study indicated that a marked disparity remained between the quantities of alcohol consumed by the sexes. Females, on average, reported drinking 93.3 per cent less than males, and even during the last occasion reported drinking 29.3 per cent less.

As one would expect, reported experience of alcohol-related consequences was generally consistent with levels of reported alcohol consumption. Some consequences, such as hangovers and experience of some degree of intoxication, were commonplace and this is hardly surprising in view of the fact that such high levels of alcohol consumption were reported. As shown in *Table 13*, while various consequences had been quite widely experienced, very few respondents reported either having been worried about their drinking (5.7 per cent of males who had tasted alcohol and 3.5 per cent of females) or reported that, in general terms, they had experienced alcohol-related problems (7.9 per cent of males and 4.4 per cent of females). These results are consistent with the view expressed by the Interdepartmental Committee on Liquor Licensing in Scotland (Clayson 1972) that drunkenness is very widely accepted in Scotland. Indeed widespread experience of some degree of intoxication appears inevitable, 21.3 per cent of males and 13.8 per cent of females supplying details of their last drinking occasion reported that they then consumed more than the equivalent of either four pints of beer or eight single glasses of wine or spirits. In fact a more meaningful comment on the females might be made in relation to those 21.8 per cent consuming more than three pints of beer or six single glasses of wine or spirits. Such a level might be more appropriate, since females are more affected by a given amount of alcohol than are males (Camberwell Council on Alcoholism 1980; Thorley 1982). As noted above, 10.9 per cent of males and 6.3 per cent of females reported having experienced ten or more of the consequences shown in *Table 13*.

This again is consistent with more general evidence of the recent substantial increase in the prevalence of alcohol-related problems amongst females (Shaw 1980). One could be justified in speculating that if this pattern persisted females would in future be likely to comprise approximately 37 per cent of those seeking help from agencies catering for problem drinkers. During 1980 approximately 28 per cent of mental hospital admissions for alcohol dependence and alcoholic psychosis in the survey area (the Lothian Health Board) were females (Scottish Home and Health Department 1981).

One of the most striking features of the results reported in this chapter was the relatively high degree of association between levels of alcohol, tobacco, and illicit drug use and of serious alcohol-related consequences. This conclusion is consistent with a growing body of evidence indicating that young people who use illicit drugs are likely to be relatively heavy consumers of alcohol and tobacco (e.g. Plant 1975; Thorley and Plant 1982). As noted by Erich Goode: 'People who use illegal drugs, marijuana especially, are fundamentally the same people who use alcohol and cigarettes – they are a little further along the same continuum. People who abstain from liquor and cigarettes are far less likely to use marijuana than people who smoke and/or drink.' (Goode 1972: 35.)

More recently the Advisory Council on the Misuse of Drugs noted:

'For some years it has been accepted by experts in the field that most drug misusers are not now solely dependent on one drug. The same person may be using a number of drugs and may be dependent on more than one of them. Opiate users will very often misuse barbiturates, amphetamines, hallucinogens, tranquillisers and alcohol. During the 1970s a more clearly defined group of multiple drug misusers emerged, individuals not necessarily physically dependent on any one drug, but psychologically dependent on drug misuse.'

(Advisory Council on the Misuse of Drugs 1982: 23)

Kandel, reviewing forty longitudinal studies of adolescent drug use, reached this conclusion:

'The use of marijuana and of other illicit drugs represents the later stages of involvement in drugs in a well defined sequence that starts with the use of those drugs – such as beer, wine, hard liquor, and cigarettes – that are socially acceptable by adults in our society. Although involvement follows a well defined order, not all adolescents who experience a particular stage go on to experiment with a later stage in the sequence. Only a subgroup at a particular stage are at risk for progression to the next stage. An important task for clinicians and researchers is to identify that subgroup of youths most at risk for further progression.'

(Kandel 1982: 343)

The link between drinking and smoking has also previously been noted. For example, Dight concluded that: ' . . . the best single predictor of heavy drinking is being a heavy smoker' (1976: 279).

These results indicate that a minority of the study group were highly 'substance-oriented' and that their use of alcohol, tobacco, and illicit drugs was associated. Amongst males, illicit drug use was also strongly predictive of experience of serious alcohol-related consequences.

As noted earlier in this chapter, the similarities between the sexes in relation to alcohol-related consequences outweighed the differences between them. For both sexes reporting that drinking was part of free time and that people who do not frequent bars miss a lot of fun were predictive of serious consequences, as was feeling like fighting after drinking. Amongst males, recreational drug use was a strong predictor, and amongst females regarding drinking as an important source of pleasure was predictive. These results indicate that amongst this study group, some important differences, partly motivational, remain in relation to the significance or effects of alcohol for the sexes.

The data about illicit drug use collected in the initial phase of this study were extremely limited at the request of some of the co-operating school authorities. No information was obtained on the frequency or level of drug ingestion, or on the presence or scale of dependence (if any) upon drugs.

Even so, these initial data indicate that at least casual experimentation with illicit drugs was by no means uncommon amongst the study group. In addition, such experimentation was clearly associated with the use of alcohol and tobacco, and in particular was positively associated with experience of relatively serious alcohol-related consequences. These results identify fairly clearly a subgroup of young males and females who appear to be 'at risk' in relation to their levels of substance use and whose fortunes will be of particular interest in Chapters 8 and 9.

These results are purely descriptive. Whether or not the data described above proved to be indicative of future patterns of alcohol use and misuse is the concern of the third wave of this study. While these initial results are of some intrinsic interest, it is possible that they may reflect transient rather than persisting patterns of behaviour. For example, it is possible that 15–16-year-old females are more socially precocious or 'mature' than are their male counterparts. If this is so, it is possible that three years hence there might be a greater disparity between the self-reported alcohol consumption and experience of associated consequences of the sexes. In fact, the prognosis for the females may not be very good. As noted by Smart: '. . . much *male* problem drinking is not permanent. Female problem drinking seems far more so. The light-hearted roistering of males frequently dissipates with few remaining problems. Problem drinking among young females does not usually have the same happy result' (Smart 1976a: 61).

These results indicated very clearly that an identifiable minority of respondents of either sex were drinking heavily even by 'adult' standards, and that such high levels of alcohol consumption were positively associated with a constellation of consequences, some of which may reasonably be acknowledged as problems. These initial results serve as a base against which one may assess the data presented below. In relation to the implications of the initial phase of this venture for alcohol education, these preliminary results are depressing.

4 The Main Follow-up

The second phase of this study was largely carried out as a consistency check. This is described in Appendix 3. The third phase was of far greater importance, being the means whereby the original aims of this follow-up study were to be tested. It involved seeking out and attempting to reinterview the original 1,036 respondents, all of whom had left school and were aged 19 and 20. This part of the study was undertaken between 21 March and 2 September, 1983. Information was collected by a direct interview and not, as in the two earlier phases, by a self-completed questionnaire. The interview involved the administration of a standard schedule by trained interviewers. Twenty-eight people implemented this fieldwork.

The interview schedule took between thirty minutes and one hour to complete. It elicited information about the following topics: (a) alcohol consumption; (b) alcohol-related consequences; (c) tobacco smoking; (d) illicit drug use; (e) employment/unemployment histories since leaving school; (f) perceptions of current job status/prospects; (g) criminal records; (h) parental drinking habits; (i) biographical details, e.g. marital status, income, educational qualifications, housing conditions; (j) other biographical information.

The schedule included eighty-three questions, some of which were quite complex. Full details of this instrument are provided in Appendix 2.

PRE-TESTING AND PILOTING

The interview schedule was pretested during autumn, 1982 with ten members of the staff of the University of Edinburgh. No major difficulties were encountered and piloting was conducted by the twenty-eight interviewers.

Fieldwork procedures were piloted during January and February, 1983. Each interviewer had been familiarized with the schedule during two training sessions. During these sessions interviewers took turns in conducting a trial interview, and responding to one. Piloting was carried out by each interviewer conducting two interviews with people of their own sex aged 19 or 20. Respondents were contacted in any manner since the aim of piloting was to test the interview rather than the follow-up procedure. Each of the fifty-four completed schedules was carefully checked and only when these had been satisfactorily completed did the main fieldwork commence. Only minor modifications were made to the original schedule.

THE MAIN FIELDWORK

Interviewers were supplied with lists of respondents whom they were to attempt to contact and interview. Initially interviewers, sixteen females and twelve males, were provided with lists of individuals of the same sex as themselves. This was because some evidence has indicated that people are more willing to disclose their alcohol consumption to interviewers of the same sex (Pernanen 1974; Cosper 1969).

To facilitate ease of contact, each interviewer was given a list of respondents living within as restricted an area as possible.

Response

Nineteen respondents (1.8 per cent) refused to co-operate with this part of the study and a further fifty-eight (5.6 per cent) could not be traced. Of the latter, thirty-four were not located because they had not provided their names or addresses when initially contacted during 1979 and 1980. Fifteen of the remaining non-contacts were not traced since they had moved away from their original address and could not be located. Two males had died. There was no evidence to suggest that either of these deaths was in any way alcohol or drug related. Ten individuals, all living overseas or in relatively distant locations, completed the interview schedules themselves and returned these by mail. A total of 957 of the original study group of 1,036 individuals were interviewed. This constituted a net response rate of 92.4 per cent. The overall pattern of response is shown in *Table 20*.

The level of response obtained by 1983 fieldwork was close to that originally hoped for on the basis of piloting. It was, however, higher than expected. An earlier two-year follow-up study of drinking habits

Table 20 Response to the third phase of the study

response	males		females		total	
	n	%	n	%*	n	%
refusals	6	1.2	13	2.3	19	1.8
non-contacts	39	8.1	19	3.4	58	5.6
died	2	0.4	—	—	2	0.2
successfully interviewed	437	90.3	520	94.2	957	92.4
total	484	100.0	552	99.9	1,036	100.0

*calculated to the nearest decimal point

in the Edinburgh area had achieved a net response rate of only 71 per cent (Plant 1979a). The 92.4 per cent rate achieved in the present study compared favourably with the rates of panel retention achieved by other comparable follow-up studies. A review by Josephson and Rosen (1978) cited seven follow-up studies of illicit drug use that were conducted in the USA. The successful follow-up rates of these investigations ranged from 44 per cent to 94 per cent, with an average of 82 per cent. Only one of these studies (related to Vietnam veterans) achieved a response rate greater than that of the present study (Robins 1974, 1978). Donovan, Jessor, and Jessor (1983) obtained a response rate of 94 per cent in their follow-up study of young drinkers. This rate may have been enhanced by the fact that those who did co-operate with the study were each paid $10.

The response rates of British general population alcohol surveys have recently been reviewed by Crawford (1984). This indicated that the average response rate achieved by seventeen studies was 78.5 per cent. A recent follow-up study of males in two areas of Ontario produced response rates of 44 per cent and 61 per cent (Giesbrecht, Conroy, and Hobbs 1984). In addition two recent single-phase Dutch alcohol surveys produced response rates of 72 per cent and 76 per cent (Garretsen and Knibbe 1984).

Although 957 respondents were interviewed, some did not answer all of the questions that were put to them. Accordingly the totals presented in relation to this phase vary from item to item.

Occupation

Twelve per cent of the study group were unemployed or on the government Youth Opportunities Programme. This constitutes 19.2 per cent of those who were economically active.* During July, 1983 the
*excluding housewives and students

overall unemployment rate in the Lothian Region was the same as that for Britain as a whole, 12.1 per cent (Manpower Services Commission 1984a). Amongst young people in the United Kingdom the unemployment rate was higher than for the overall work-force. In July, 1983, 23.4 per cent of males and 16.9 per cent of females aged 20–4 were unemployed. The corresponding figures for males and females aged 18–19 were 28.7 per cent and 21.6 per cent respectively (Department of Employment 1983). Thus the level of unemployment amongst the study group was rather lower than that for their age-group throughout the United Kingdom. A quarter were in full-time education and virtually all of the others were employed.

Table 21 The occupations of the study group during 1983

occupation	males		females	
	n	%	n	%
full-time employment	244	56.3	296	59.7
part-time employment	9	2.1	13	2.6
full-time education	106	24.5	122	24.6
unemployed	61	14.1	42	8.5
Youth Opportunities Programme	3	0.7	7	1.4
housewife/mother	—	—	10	2.0
other	10	2.3	6	1.2
total	433	100.0	496	100.0

The proportion of the study group who were in full-time education was significantly higher than that amongst the general population. The 1981 Census had shown that 17.6 per cent of males and 16.4 per cent of females aged 19 and 20 in Lothian were students (Registrar General Scotland 1982: I, 14).

As *Table 21* shows, patterns of employment and unemployment amongst males and females were virtually identical.

Marital Status

The marital status of the study group is shown in *Table 22*.

Only one male and eighteen females reported being married. As *Table 22* shows, five males and seven females were cohabiting. This is a much lower rate of marriage than anticipated. In 1981, two years before this fieldwork had been conducted, the Census had shown that 7.8 per cent of males and 18.2 per cent of females aged 19 and 20 in the Lothian

Region were married (Registrar General Scotland 1982: I, 28). One male and nineteen female respondents reported that they were engaged to be married. Even if these were taken into account the proportion of the study group who were married remains strikingly lower than that in the general population.

Table 22 The marital status of the study group

status	males*		females	
	n	%	n	%
unmarried	432	98.6	488	95.1
married	1	0.2	18	3.5
cohabiting	5	1.1	7	1.4
total	438	99.9	513	100.0

*calculated to the nearest decimal point

Social Class

During the first two phases of this study respondents had been asked to classify their parents' occupations as either 'manual' or 'non-manual'. As noted in Chapter 3, this produced a pattern closely in accordance with that for the general population of the Lothian Region.

When interviewed during 1983, more detailed information was elicited about parental occupations. This is elaborated in Appendix 2. From the details thus obtained, parental social class was later coded in accordance with the Registrar General's classification. Status was ascribed in relation to that of the male head of each respondent's household. In the small minority of cases in which there was no male, classification was made in relation to female head of household. The social-class background of the study group is shown in *Table 23*.

There was a small, but significant, difference between the social-class backgrounds of the study group and that of the overall population of the Lothian Region as indicated by the 1981 Census. This is a different conclusion from that produced by the initial wave of data collection. In fact the study group were marginally more likely than the general population to come from non-manual backgrounds (49.5 per cent compared with 45.6 per cent). This slight difference may partly, but only partly, explain why so few of the study group were married and why so many were students.

It must be noted that census data, unlike those collected by the third wave of this study, were based upon self-completed questionnaires. In addition to those classified according to the Registrar General's social-class group, approximately 24 per cent of households recorded in the census for the Lothian Region were assigned to other categories due to the fact that their heads were retired or in the armed forces, or were inadequately described. A slightly different procedure was adopted in the present study since retired household heads were classified in accordance with their last job. None was inadequately described.

Table 23 The social-class background of the study group

Registrar General's social class group	the study group		Lothian Region (1981 census)
	n	%*	%*
I professional/managerial	93	9.9	7.9
II intermediate non-manual	234	25.0	23.7
III skilled non-manual	137	14.6	14.0
IV skilled manual	300	32.0	32.9
V partly skilled manual	139	14.8	15.7
VI unskilled manual	34	3.6	5.7
total	937	99.9	99.9

*calculated to the nearest decimal place

The study group clearly differed significantly from the overall population of the Lothian Region in relation to marital and occupational status (including unemployment) and, to a lesser degree, to social class. This must be borne in mind when considering the overall results of this study. Even so, much of the analysis that follows is concerned with the differences in substance use between specific subgroups, such as those from different social-class backgrounds or those in different work settings. Moreover it is emphasized that although the study group did differ in certain respects from the general population, it still covered the complete range of social class backgrounds. As *Table 23* indicates, the difference in backgrounds of the study group and the regional population, though statistically significant, was very small.

The main results of the third phase of this study are presented in the next four chapters. These relate to the two primary aims that this exercise sought to achieve.

5 Alcohol Consumption and Alcohol-related Consequences

This chapter and the three that follow it present the main results of the 1983 data. Where in the authors' opinion it is helpful, these results are also briefly compared with baseline information collected during 1979/80.

ALCOHOL CONSUMPTION PATTERNS

The study group had been aged 15 and 16 when first examined in 1979 and 1980. They were aged 19 and 20 when interviewed during 1983.

During the initial wave of data collection respondents had provided details of their alcohol consumption during the previous week and on their last drinking occasion. Parallel information was elicited during 1983. The results of this comparison are shown in *Table 24*.

The average level of alcohol consumed by males had increased substantially during the 1979/80 to 1983 period. However, there was virtually no change in that reported by females.

A detailed picture of the previous week's alcohol consumption of the study group is provided in *Table 25*.

The highest previous week's consumption reported by any male was 134 units. This is equivalent to 50 pints of beer or approximately three bottles of spirits.

The average amount of alcohol consumed by males, 20.5 units, was significantly higher than that consumed by females, 9.4 units. In addition a quarter of the females reported not having consumed any alcohol in the previous week. This is twice the proportion of male non-drinkers. Only seven males and thirteen females reported not having drunk alcohol in the past two years.

Table 24 Changes in self-reported alcohol consumption (1979/80 to 1983)

alcohol consumption	males	females
	units	units
x̄ [a]previous week's consumption (all respondents)		
1979/80	17.8	9.2
1983	23.6	9.0
% change 1979/80 to 1983	+33.0%	−1.7%
x̄ consumption on last drinking occasion (all respondents)		
1979/80	4.9	4.1
1983	6.2	3.4
% change 1979/80 to 83	+17.0%	−17.1%

[a]average

Table 25 Previous week's self-reported alcohol consumption

units consumed	males*		females**	
	n	%	n	%
no alcohol consumed	58	13.4	132	26.6
1–10	119	27.5	258	52.0
11–20	100	23.1	72	14.5
21–30	52	12.0	22	4.4
31–50	66	15.2	10	2.0
51–70	19	4.4	0	0.0
71–100	12	2.8	2	0.4
101or more	7	1.6	0	0.0
total	433	100.0	496	99.9***

*x̄ (all respondents) = 20.5 units, standard deviation = 22 units, range = 0–134 units
**x̄ (all respondents) = 6.6 units, standard deviation = 9.4 units, range = 0–100 units
***calculated to nearest decimal place
Note x̄ of those who drank in previous week: males = 23.6 units; females = 9.0 units

The two sexes did not differ markedly as to the location of their last drinking occasion. These are shown in *Table 26*.

Females (21 per cent) were more likely than males (12.6 per cent) to report having last consumed alcohol in their own or somebody else's home. Males were slightly more likely than females to have drunk in a

Table 26 Location of most recent drink

location	males		females	
	n	%	*n*	%
bar	218	50.5	218	43.6
licensed club	54	12.5	55	11.0
disco/dance	44	10.2	63	12.6
hotel	33	7.7	29	5.8
own home	25	5.8	53	10.6
home of friend	24	5.6	44	8.8
home of relative	5	1.2	8	1.6
other	28	6.5	30	6.0
total	431	100.0	500	100.0

bar. Even so, the overall pattern of the location of drinking did not differ significantly between the sexes.

Drinking Companions

Respondents were asked with whom they had been on their last drinking occasion. Responses are shown in *Table 27*.

Only one major difference emerged between the patterns reported by respondents of either sex. Males were much more likely to report

Table 27 Companions during last drinking occasion

companions (in overall rank order)	males		females	
	n	%	*n*	%
friends of both sexes	121	28.1	161	32.3
friend/s of same sex	174	40.4	103	20.7
spouse/cohabitee/boyfriend★/ girlfriend★	26	6.0	79	15.9
parents/stepparents/guardians	21	4.9	50	10.0
friend/s opposite sex	16	3.7	43	8.6
siblings	25	5.8	28	5.6
workmates	19	4.4	21	4.2
other relatives	18	4.2	12	2.4
no companion – drinking alone	11	2.5	1	0.2
total	431	100.0	498	99.9

★of opposite sex

Table 28 Alcohol-related consequences reported by the study group

consequences	males (n = 437)		females (n = 520)	
	n	%	n	%
a) DRUNKENNESS				
i) have had 'a really terrible hangover' in past six months	152	34.8	117	22.5
ii) excessive sweating following drinking in past three months	33	7.5	14	2.7
iii) hands trembled in morning after drinking in past three months	51	11.7	30	5.8
iv) unable to hold a glass due to shakes in past three months	17	3.9	4	0.8
v) have had morning drink to relax, or to 'cure a hangover' in past 3 months	19	4.3	8	1.5
vi) have felt restless/irritable being without a drink in the past three months	18	4.1	13	2.5
b) HEALTH				
i) ulcer				
has stomach ulcer attributed by respondent to alcohol	0	—	1	0.2
has stomach ulcer attributed by other person to alcohol	2	0.5	1	0.2
ii) gastritis				
has gastritis attributed by respondent to alcohol	1	0.2	1	0.2
has gastritis attributed by other person to alcohol	0	—	2	0.4
iii) has had alcohol-related accident in past two years attributed by respondent to alcohol	21	4.8	2	0.4
attributed by other person to alcohol	1	0.2	—	—
iv) overdose (parasuicide)				
has taken overdose attributed by respondent to alcohol	2	0.5	4	0.8
has taken overdose attributed by other person to alcohol	—	—	—	—
c) SOCIAL (INCLUDING PUBLIC ORDER)				
i) has been in argument at home about own drinking in past two years	72	16.5	14	2.7
ii) has been involved in violent arguments at home attributed by respondent to alcohol	4	0.9	—	—
attributed by other person to alcohol	2	0.5	1	0.2
iii) domestic break-up threatened attributed by respondent to alcohol	25	5.7	13	2.5
attributed by other person to alcohol	1	0.2	1	0.2

consequences	males (n = 437)		females (n = 520)	
	n	%	n	%
iv) respondent asked to leave a place				
attributed by respondent to alcohol	68	15.6	15	2.9
attributed by other person to alcohol	8	1.8	2	0.4
v) have been in a fight while drinking in				
past two years	108	24.7	15	2.9
vi) have received or inflicted injury in a fight				
while drinking in past two years	66	15.1	7	1.3
vii) have experienced financial difficulties				
due to drinking	39	8.9	9	1.7
viii) regret having done the following while drinking:				
said something	218	49.9	207	39.8
been sexually involved with someone	93	21.3	33	6.3
been loud and noisy	170	38.9	109	21.0
been destructive and aggressive	73	16.7	12	2.3
been weepy and tearful	32	7.3	152	29.2
become pregnant/got someone pregnant	4	0.9	4	0.8
been sick/passed out in presence of others	141	32.3	115	22.1
unable to perform well	89	20.4	17	3.3
unable to recall events	177	40.5	120	23.1
committed misdemeanour/crime	77	17.6	8	1.5
ix) have been in trouble with police or convicted of an offence attributed by				
respondent to alcohol	26	5.9	6	1.2
attributed by other person to alcohol	4	0.9	1	0.2
d) WORK/EDUCATION				
i) absent from work/education attributed				
by respondent to alcohol	53	12.1	26	5.0
attributed by other person to alcohol	7	1.6	6	1.2
ii) late for work/education attributed by				
respondent to alcohol	70	16.0	23	4.4
attributed by other person to alcohol	9	2.1	1	0.2
iii) have left a job attributed by respondent				
to alcohol	0	—	1	0.2
attributed by other person to alcohol	1	0.2	0	—
e) RECEIPT OF HELP FOR DRINKING PROBLEMS FROM:				
i) GP/other doctor apart from psychiatrist	1	0.2	0	—
ii) psychiatrist/psychologist	0	—	1	0.2
iii) Council on Alcoholism/Drinkwatchers/AA or other group	0	—	0	—
iv) teacher/minister of religion	0	—	0	—
v) family/friends	0	—	0	—
vi) social worker	0	—	0	—
vii) other person/agency	0	—	0	—

having been drinking with a friend or friends of the same sex than were females. The overwhelming majority of respondents reported having been in the company of others during their last drinking occasion. In addition, predictably, most of these had been with friends rather than with relatives.

ALCOHOL-RELATED CONSEQUENCES

A considerable part of the interview was concerned with alcohol-related consequences. For convenience these may be subdivided into the following five categories: drunkenness, health, social (including public order), work/education, and seeking help for a drinking problem. As shown in Appendix 2, most of these consequences were the subject of several questions. These related to the frequency or recentness of each consequence and to whether or not anyone had reason to link the consequence with the respondent's drinking. A concise and selective summary of the responses to these questions is presented in *Table 28* on pages 62–3.

Alcohol-related consequences were considerably more common amongst males than amongst females, as might be expected from the males' higher consumption levels. The only exceptions to this general trend were the consequences related to health, where on a number of items, females reported a higher level of consequences (e.g. having taken an overdose for which alcohol was said to be partially responsible). However, the numbers involved are extremely small, and it is doubtful if any importance can be placed upon them.

A substantial proportion of the respondents reported having had a 'really terrible hangover' within the last six months (34.6 per cent for males, 22.7 per cent for females). However, the more serious consequences of high alcohol consumption (for example, having had a drink in the morning to cure a hangover) were relatively rare, particularly amongst females. Social and/or legal consequences of alcohol consumption were extremely rare amongst females but quite common amongst the males. For example, 16.4 per cent of the males had had arguments at home about their own drinking within the last two years, 15.5 per cent had been asked to leave a place because of alcoholic intoxication, 24.6 per cent had been involved in a fight while drinking within the last two years (for 15 per cent of the males this fight had resulted in an injury), and 8.9 per cent had experienced financial difficulties due to drinking.

More common were expressed regrets after drinking. In particular both sexes reported a high frequency of regretting having said something while drinking, having been loud and noisy during a drinking bout, vomiting or passing out in the presence of other people, and subsequently being unable to recall events. Some of these regrets were more common amongst males: having been sexually involved with someone while drinking, having been destructive and aggressive, being unable to perform well, and having committed a misdemeanour or crime. The only regret more common amongst females was having been weepy and tearful during drinking.

Occupational consequences were relatively rare, although 12 per cent of males had been absent from work because of drinking, and 15.9 per cent of males had been late for work because of drinking. The corresponding figures for females were 5.1 per cent and 4.5 per cent. Apart from this, drinking seemed to have very few consequences for work or education.

Despite the relatively high level of some of these consequences, including serious ones such as a misdemeanour or crime attributed to drinking, it is emphasized that only one male and four females reported having sought help for drinking problems.

As noted above many of the 'consequences' of drinking were not serious. Adopting a similar procedure to that employed in Chapter 3, a scale of 'serious problems' was compiled. This consisted of the following twelve alcohol-related consequences, which the authors judged to be non-trivial; severe shakes, severe hangover, drinking upon waking to cure a hangover, having had an alcohol-related accident, having taken an 'alcohol-related overdose', hitting somebody after drinking, fighting after drinking, alcohol-related absence from work, alcohol-related leaving of job, financial difficulties, criminal conviction, and conviction for drunken driving. The levels of such serious problems reportedly experienced by the study group are shown in *Table 29* on page 64.

Altogether 65 per cent of males and 43.2 per cent of females reported having experienced at least one serious alcohol-related consequence. This difference between the sexes was statistically significant.

DISCUSSION

It is not surprising that the patterns of alcohol consumption and alcohol-related consequences of the study group had changed since 1979/80.

Table 29 Experience of serious alcohol-related consequences

number of problems	males		females	
	n	%	n	%
0	153	35.1	288	56.8
1	126	28.9	171	33.7
2	73	16.7	31	6.1
3	39	8.9	9	1.8
4	20	4.6	4	0.8
5	17	3.9	3	0.6
6	2	0.5	0	—
7	3	0.7	1	0.2
8	3	0.7	0	—
total	436	100.0	507	100.0

During that period respondents had all left school and were at least three years older than when first included in the study.

Alcohol Consumption

The levels of alcohol consumption reported by the study group during 1983 were very similar to those reported by Wilson (1980b) in relation to people aged 20–7 in surveys of United Kingdom drinking habits that were undertaken in autumn, 1978. This is shown in *Table 30*.

The mean levels of alcohol consumption amongst those in the present study who had drunk in the previous week were not very different from those noted by Wilson in Scotland during 1978. In addition the level of

Table 30 Comparison of alcohol consumption in the present study with United Kingdom data obtained during 1978 (drinkers only)

	average previous week's consumption (in units)	
	males	females
present study (1983)	23.6	9.0
Scotland★ (1978)	26.2	7.7
England and Wales★ (1978)	26.6	9.7
Northern Ireland★ (1978)	18.9	7.0

★figures refer to 20–7 age group

consumption noted amongst females in the present study also closely resembled that of Wilson's females who were interviewed in England and Wales in 1978. These differences are trivial and the only subgroup in *Table 30* that was markedly different were Wilson's men in Northern Ireland who were drinking far less than their counterparts in Britain.

With reference to *Table 24*, it is interesting that while consumption amongst males in the present study had risen since 1979/80, that of females had remained almost unchanged. As noted in Chapter 3 the Canadian researcher Smart (1979a) suggested that 'youthful roistering' amongst males was more commonplace than amongst females. These results in fact suggest that in the present study group the reverse may have been true.

During the course of the four years or so between the first and third waves of data collection, the study group had all achieved the legal age to drink alcohol in public bars. When first examined in 1979/80 the majority reported last consuming alcohol in their own homes or in the homes of others. By 1983 for both sexes the bar had become the most commonly reported location of last drink.

Several surveys have provided an indication of the extent to which British drinking takes place in bars. One survey of Scottish drinking habits in 1972 concluded that 73 per cent of past week's drinking amongst males had occurred in public bars and that amongst females the corresponding level was 44 per cent (Dight 1976). A 1978 survey of drinking habits in England and Wales showed that 63 per cent of previous week's alcohol consumption amongst men and 44 per cent of that amongst women occurred in bars (Wilson 1980a). In addition both studies showed that heavy drinkers of either sex were those who consume the highest proportion of their alcohol in bars. This conclusion is supported in the present study in relation to males, but not to females. Males who had consumed alcohol in a bar or hotel had on average drunk 22.9 units in the previous week compared with only 17.1 units amongst males who had last drunk elsewhere. Previous week's alcohol consumption amongst females did not differ significantly when the same comparison was made.

Rachel *et al.* (1980) summarized five American literature reviews of youthful alcohol use:

'None of the five reviews conclude that adolescent drinking has become heavier or more intense in recent years. Blane and Hewitt (1977) believe that the data do not indicate that drinking frequency has increased. Nor do they conclude that there were significant differences in the proportions of adolescents drinking to intoxication between 1966–75 and earlier years.

Without exception, all five reviews concluded that more boys than girls were drinkers during early adolescent years. However, considerable disagreement is apparent among the reviewers on whether the difference in prevalence between boys and girls is narrowing.'

(Rachel *et al.* 1980: 4)

This view is reinforced by several other authors (e.g. Zucker and Harford 1983).

Polich (1979) has reviewed four American general-population alcohol surveys which were carried out by Louis Harris and Associates (Harris 1975). Polich commented thus:

' . . . there remains a wide discrepancy between the sexes despite the widespread public impression that male and female drinking practices have been converging in recent years. Males of all ages are much more likely than females to be drinkers (i.e. to have consumed any alcoholic beverage in the past 30 days), and if they do drink, their frequency of drinking is likely to be two or three times as great. (These results hold up both for the 18- to 20-year-old group and for the 21- to 24-year-old group). When one considers *quantity* of consumption on a drinking day, these disparities remain.'

(Polich 1979: 67)

Polich also notes that by any criteria young males are the heaviest drinking subgroup of the population.

Ratcliff and Burkhart have suggested that there remain differences in the sexes' expectations of alcohol: ' . . . women tend to drink to enhance social pleasures, whereas men expect a greater degree of aggressive arousal and social deviance when drinking' (1984: 26).

As noted in Chapter 3 the level of alcohol use in the present study group was higher than that noted by Rachel and colleagues and by other American researchers. These studies indicate that as young people become older their alcohol consumption increases. This is consistent with the experience of the males, but not of the females, in the present investigation.

A considerable body of survey data related to the drinking habits of young people has been produced in Finland (e.g. Ahlstrom 1975, 1979, 1981, 1982a, 1982b). Sulkunen (1981) has suggested that the big decline in that country in the number of abstainers is attributable not so much to changed living conditions as to a 'generation gap'.

'What came to be called the Wet Generation was found to include very few abstainers, and this did not only depend on the fact that this generation came to live in different circumstances from those of its parents. Among those in the age group 20–29 years in 1976 the abstinence rate did not vary by occupation or even by sex, the two socio-demographic factors that most clearly distinguished abstainers from drinkers in the older population.'

(Sulkunen 1981: 1)

A 1976 Finnish survey by Simpura (1978) showed that males in the 20–9 age group had drunk three times as much alcohol as their female counterparts. This is similar to the analysis of previous week's drinking shown in *Table 25*. However, Simpura also found that fewer than 30 per cent of those of either sex aged 20–9 consumed alcohol each week. This is a much lower level than that noted in the present study.

Finnish data, like those from the United States, have indicated that the percentage of non-drinkers falls steadily between the ages of 12 and 18 and that during the 1960s and 1970s the percentage of young people of specific ages who did not drink fell considerably (e.g. Ahlstrom 1979; Sulkunen 1981). Similar conclusions have been reached in relation to other countries (Armyr, Elmer, and Herz 1982; Addiction Research Foundation 1982). Smart and Murray (1981) reviewed trends in alcohol use amongst young people in Australia, Canada, Denmark, Finland, Mexico, Norway, Sweden, and the United States. They concluded that levels of drinking had peaked and that alcohol consumption appeared to have stabilized or decreased in many countries since 1975–76. As noted in Chapter 1 per capita alcohol consumption in the United Kingdom declined slightly during the present study, as did some of the indicators of officially recorded alcohol misuse.

The Consequences of Drinking

In Chapter 3 it was noted that at the ages of 15 and 16 the sexes did not differ very much as to the consequences of their drinking. By the ages of 19 and 20 a greater gulf had opened up between males and females in this respect. This conclusion is consistent with a large body of data from several countries that shows levels of alcohol-related problems to be far higher amongst men than amongst women (Cahalan, Cisin, and

Crossley 1969; Edwards, Chandler, and Hensman 1972; Cartwright, Shaw, and Spratley 1978; Donovan and Jessor 1978; Morgan 1979; Smart and Murray 1981; Stacey 1981; Hibell 1981).

In spite of this, as in other studies, alcohol-related consequences were by no means a male prerogative. Although females were drinking much less than males a substantial minority reported being intoxicated or experiencing other alcohol-related consequences. Amongst males 65 per cent reported one or more 'serious' consequences while 43 per cent of females reported such consequences. The difference, though statistically significant, is by no means as great as that suggested by variations in alcohol consumption. Males, though drinking on average three times as much as females, were only about 50 per cent more likely than females to have experienced one or more 'serious' consequences. Males were, however, roughly three times more likely than females to report having experienced three or more serious consequences. Curiously, females, as shown by *Table 28*, were more likely than males to report having received help for a drinking problem. It is widely noted that females may experience alcohol-related problems at lower levels of alcohol consumption than men (Greenblatt and Schuckit 1976; Kalant 1980). An earlier study of alcohol-dependent patients in Edinburgh had indicated that females reported experiencing similar levels of consequences to those reported by males even though females drank much less (Plant and Plant 1979).

The 3:1 ratio of males:females experiencing three or more consequences is broadly compatible with the sex ratio amongst psychiatric hospital in-patients being treated for alcohol dependence in Scotland. This ratio is not compatible with the fact that only one male and four females reported having received help for alcohol problems. These are very small numbers and relate only to young people in one locality. Even so, it is certain that psychiatric hospital statistics do not include many problem drinkers who seek help from other agencies. Women may generally be less likely than men to seek help from psychiatric hospital-based alcohol units, preferring instead to contact other agencies. As shown by *Table 28*, most of the helping agents cited by females were not psychiatrists or psychologists.

The health implications of youthful heavy drinking are often unclear. Some obviously harmful consequences were reported by some of the people in this study. In spite of this many possible adverse long-term consequences are unlikely to become apparent amongst people in their early twenties. The overwhelming majority of alcohol-related liver cirrhosis deaths and hospital admissions for alcohol dependence involve middle-aged and elderly people. Youthful heavy drinking may be setting the scene for such severe and chronic consequences in later life. In 1979 a special committee of the Royal College of Psychiatrists advanced the following advice:

'We would suggest that an intake of four pints of beer a day, four doubles of spirits or one standard-sized bottle of wine, constitute reasonable guidelines for the upper limit of drinking. It is unwise to make a habit of drinking even at these levels, and anyone driving a vehicle should not drink at all before driving . . . different people react differently to the same dose of any drug, and such additional factors as body weight, for instance, must of course influence the response to a given dose. The way in which daily quantity is spaced out during the day will influence its effects.'

(Royal College of Psychiatrists 1979: 140)

A similar view has been voiced by Thorley:

'in the last ten years it has become clear from a number of international studies that a man of average weight who drinks on a regular daily basis more than ten units (80 grams) of ethanol, equivalent to five pints of average beer, has an increased likelihood of future alcohol-related illnesses, social problems and legal offences . . . women's threshold of regular excessive consumption is even lower than men's, being set at about six units a day, or three pints of average beer.'

(Thorley 1982: 45)

Seven males in the present study had consumed at least 101 units of alcohol in the week preceding interview. In addition two females had consumed over 70 units of alcohol. These individuals were drinking amounts which bordered on or exceeded the 'upper limit of drinking' advocated by the Royal College of Psychiatrists.

In conclusion, these data, like those in Chapter 3, indicate that the drinking of the overwhelming majority of respondents was not sufficient to cause concern. A minority, however, had experienced serious consequences. These results certainly do not support the frequently voiced media claim that alcohol dependence or even serious harm due to drinking amongst young people has reached catastrophic levels. On the contrary, it is the authors' view that the level of even serious consequences amongst the study group was not unduly high.

Moreover, since individual drinking patterns frequently change, it cannot be concluded that the experience of even serious consequences, though regrettable in itself, necessarily has sinister long-term implications. It is well documented that young single people generally drink more heavily than do older, married, individuals. In addition such youthful drinking is frequently accompanied by consequences which do not persist.

Polich, reviewing American data, concluded that:

'serious consequences of drinking are rare in the general population, since in no instance does any item reach much above 5 per cent of the same. The fact that the rates for these events are individually low, however, does not imply that alcohol problems are infrequent when considered in the aggregate. The reason is that the events are not all concentrated in a small group of individuals with chronic problems (such as alcoholism). Many persons experience just one such consequence during a three-year period. Thus, those who reported incidents of work impairment during the period are not necessarily the same people as those who were hospitalized or involved in an accident. To a considerable extent, adverse consequences tend to be disjointed events, often devoid of a pattern or linkage that would suggest persistent, continuous drinking or alcohol dependence.'

(Polich 1979: 74)

This view has been amplified by Blane who has commented thus:

'Frequent heavy drinking is not chronic in the sense of being continuous nor pervasive in the sense of affecting all spheres of the individual's life. Heavy drinking may occur several times a week, and the consequences of drinking may indeed affect a person's life, but intake is episodic and occurs within a more-or-less conventionally ordered lifestyle. More critically, perhaps, alcohol is not a guiding principle in the frequent heavy drinker's lifestyle. Drinking episodes are self-limiting and circumscribed events that occur independently of other significant life events. Important for the moment, they recede into the background of one's existence as other activities come to the fore. . . . Another aspect of frequent heavy drinking is that it appears largely as a self-limiting condition that moderates with age, probably peaking at 18–20 years of age and declining steadily thereafter.'

(Blane 1979: 9)

Blane has provided another comment which is compatible with the results obtained by the present study:

'Concerning the observation that frequent heavy drinking is a self-limiting condition for a majority of young adults who exhibit it, most of the research cited earlier indicates a steady decrease in the proportions of individuals who fall into frequent heavy drinking categories at each successive age level. The trend is most clearly delineated for men. Women, on the other hand, may maintain or increase frequent heavy drinking as they get older, but the absolute level never appears to be high. For both men and women, the frequency of drinking occasions increases with age; for men, the quantity per occasion declines, whereas for women, it may stay the same or increase.

The factors underlying declines in frequent heavy drinking among men are not at all understood. General explanations like "burning out" or "settling down" are not satisfactory. One alternative is that frequent heavy drinking has symbolic associations with significant developmental markers of young adulthood, such as, for example, establishment and consolidation of adult identity. Once these developmental tasks have been accomplished and the stage in which they are rooted passes, symbolic connections to heavy drinking become weaker and less compelling.'

(Blane 1979: 28)

Blane's interpretation is a plausible one. Earlier Scottish research by Jahoda and Crammond (1972) and by Davies and Stacey (1972) has shown how attitudes to alcohol develop and change amongst young people. In particular Davies and Stacey have indicated that, especially amongst males, alcohol consumption is viewed as a hallmark of maturity.

It is possible that levels of alcohol consumption amongst females may have already peaked by the age of 19 and 20. Firm conclusions about this may only be drawn if a further follow-up of this group is conducted in the future. Survey data collected in the four countries of the United Kingdom during 1978 have led to the conclusion that the heaviest alcohol consumption occurs amongst the 20–7 age group. This was true of both sexes. Interestingly, males in Scotland deviated from this general pattern, since alcohol consumption amongst those aged 28–37 was as high as amongst the 20–7 age group (Wilson 1980a). As Wilson notes, this is consistent with the view that in Scotland levels of youthful heavy drinking may persist longer than they do south of the border. If this is generally true the males in the present study may have embarked upon drinking patterns that might persist for nearly two decades.

6 Tobacco and Illicit Drug Use

TOBACCO SMOKING

The drug that is responsible for by far the greatest amount of health damage is tobacco. Previous research has frequently indicated that smoking and drinking habits are often related. Accordingly some basic, though very limited, information was collected about the smoking habits of the study group. Respondents were asked whether or not they ever smoked tobacco. The majority reported that they did not. The daily cigarette use of the study group is shown in *Table 31*.

Table 31 Daily cigarette smoking by the study group

number of cigarettes smoked each day	males		females	
	n	%	*n*	%
none	279	64.7	305	60.6
1 or less	17	3.9	33	6.6
2–4	11	2.6	16	3.2
5–10	37	8.6	54	10.7
11–20	72	16.7	84	16.7
21 or more	15	3.5	11	2.2
total	431	100.0	503	100.0

$\bar{x}$ of all males = 4.5 cigarettes
$\bar{x}$ of all females = 4.0 cigarettes
$\bar{x}$ of male smokers = 12.5 cigarettes
$\bar{x}$ of female smokers = 10.5 cigarettes

Females were slightly more likely than males to report that they smoked cigarettes (39.4 per cent versus 35.3 per cent). Nevertheless males on average smoked more cigarettes than did females whether all respondents, or solely those who smoke, are considered. None of these differences was, however, statistically significant.

Discussion

When first examined in 1979/80, 30 per cent of males and 37 per cent of females reported being smokers. Four years later the percentages of either sex who smoked had risen only slightly and the difference between the sexes was no longer significant. As already noted in Chapter 3 the smoking habits of the study group at the ages of 15 and 16 were very similar to those described in other British surveys (Ledwith 1983; Dobbs and Marsh 1983).

In 1983 the Royal College of Physicians published their fourth report on tobacco, *Health or Smoking?*. This summarized some of the recent evidence on tobacco smoking in the United Kingdom and concluded that amongst both young men and women the percentage of smokers was falling. In addition it was concluded that: 'The proportions of young men and women who smoke have converged and are now roughly similar' (1983: 62). The report provides a useful and authoritative source of comparative data for the results of this study.

'Few women smoked before World War II. After that time the habit became increasingly popular, so that by 1956 some 42 per cent of women aged 16 and over were smokers. . . . Until the mid 1970's the figure remained relatively constant – fluctuating between 40 per cent and 45 per cent. There is, however, a recent indication of a definite decline in the proportion of women smoking. The General Household Survey published by the Government's Office of Population Censuses and Surveys gave a figure of 38 per cent for 1976, 37 per cent for 1978 and 1980 and just 33 per cent for 1982. . . . These are encouraging findings, for the decline now seems to be affecting heavier smokers and is no longer accounted for entirely by a reduction in the number of light smokers. The percentage of women smoking more than 20 cigarettes per day was steady at 13 to 14 per cent and is now 11 per cent (1982).'

(Royal College of Physicians 1983: 61–2)

The General Household Survey cited by the Royal College of Physicians provided a considerable amount of information about smoking habits in Britain. This reinforced earlier evidence that cigarette smoking, in contrast with most other forms of psychoactive drug use, was becoming less popular. Between 1972 and 1982 the average weekly cigarette consumption per adult in Britain fell from 48 to 39, a decline of 23 per cent (Tobacco Advisory Council 1984).

The 1982 General Household Survey indicated that 41 per cent of males and 40 per cent of females aged 20–4 smoked cigarettes. The General Household Survey referred to a slightly older group than the respondents in the present study. Even so the proportion of smokers of either sex in this study was close to that noted in the 1982 national survey.

The General Household Survey also noted that amongst smokers in the 20–4 age group the average weekly cigarette consumption of males was 114 and that of females was 100 cigarettes. Referring to *Table 31* the corresponding levels for smokers in the present study were (males) 87.5 and (females) 73.5 cigarettes. These differences are to a large extent attributable to the relative youthfulness of respondents in the present study. The General Household Survey showed that amongst those in the 16–17 age group average weekly cigarette consumption per smoker was 87 for males and 76 for females.

The General Household Survey also confirmed earlier evidence (e.g. Bostock and Davies 1979) that the proportion of smokers amongst the population aged 65 and over in Scotland was 42 per cent, higher than elsewhere in Britain (Office of Population Censuses and Surveys 1984: 189–202).

In short these results indicate that the study group was smoking in much the same way as other British young people of similar age. The smoking data collected in this study were obtained in order to examine their relationship to alcohol and drug consumption and their related consequences.

ILLICIT DRUG USE

This study was initiated to investigate issues related to the use and misuse of alcohol. Even at its inception public concern was growing about the upsurge of illicit drug use. Accordingly, the first two phases of the investigation elicited an extremely limited amount of information related to illicit drug use. By the time that the third phase of the study was being planned in the autumn of 1982, public alarm about illicit drugs had reached a high level. Very little recent survey work appeared to have been carried out into United Kingdom drug use. It was decided that the third-wave interview should include some items related to illicit drugs for two main reasons. Firstly, the baseline results of this study, described in Chapter 3, had shown a high level of association between alcohol misuse and experimentation with substances such as cannabis, glues, solvents, and other illicit drugs. It was also considered that the exclusion of illicit drugs from this study would have meant missing a good opportunity to extend the scope of the investigation. Broadening the scope of the study was undertaken in order to investigate empirically an area that was characterized by un-substantiated assertions.

In devising the interview schedule the authors were constrained by conflicting pressures. The main imperative was to include items that would help to fulfil the project's original aims. The second constraint was that of producing a reasonably short interview. This important requirement necessitated the exclusion of many topics or questions which were also of interest.

It was felt that illicit drug use warranted more attention than had been accorded it in the original self-completed questionnaire. Illicit drugs remained a subsidiary aspect of the study. Consequently, approximately 6 per cent of the interview schedule was related to this topic (see Appendix 2).

Respondents were asked which drugs they had ever used. It was emphasized that such use was for 'enjoyment or out of curiosity, but *not* for medical purposes'. Respondents reporting that they had used a drug (such as cannabis or cocaine) were then asked if they had used it in the last six months and, if so, how often. All respondents who had used drugs were asked whether they had ever had financial, domestic, social (outside home), work/school, legal, or health problems connected with their drug use. Those currently using drugs were asked if they would find it hard or inconvenient to give up using the drug/drugs for a month. Finally respondents were asked if, in the past two years, they had ever used illicit drugs at the same time as alcohol.

Patterns of Illicit Drug Use

Altogether 37 per cent of males and 23.2 per cent of females reported having at some time used illicit drugs. This difference between the sexes was significant. *Table 32* shows the levels of drug use reported by the study group both in 1983 and during 1979/80.

The self-reported use of cannabis, LSD and amphetamines rose considerably for both sexes between 1979/80 and 1983. Amongst females in particular there was also an increase in the number who had used cocaine. In contrast both sexes were less likely in 1983 than they had been in 1979/80 to report having used either glues, solvents, or sleeping-tablets and tranquillizers. Opiate use remained confined to a

Table 32 Changes in self-reported illicit drug use (1979/80 to 1983)

drug	males (n = 436)				females (n = 514)			
	1979/80		1983		1979/80		1983	
	n	%	n	%	n	%	n	%
cannabis	32	7.3	152	34.9	35	6.8	114	22.2
LSD	4	0.9	25	5.7	6	1.2	13	2.5
barbiturates	5	1.1	4	0.9	7	1.4	7	1.4
Mogadon	6	1.4	6	1.4	3	0.6	8	1.6
Librium	1	0.2	3	0.7	2	0.4	3	0.6
Valium	16	3.7	17	3.9	19	3.7	11	2.1
glues/solvents	20	4.6	10	2.3	20	3.9	8	1.6
amphetamines	5	1.1	36	8.3	15	2.9	27	5.2
opium	2	0.5	4	0.9	3	0.6	1	0.2
morphine	0	—	1	0.2	1	0.2	0	—
heroin	2	0.5	3	0.7	2	0.4	3	0.6
Methadone	no data		2	0.5	no data		1	0.2
cocaine	7	1.6	10	2.3	2	0.4	10	1.9
sleeping-tablets/ tranquillizers	20	4.6	9	2.1	27	5.2	8	1.6
PCP (angel dust)	no data		1	0.2	no data		0	0.0
hallucinogenic fungi	no data		21	4.8	no data		9	1.8

small minority. Even so the numbers reportedly having at some time used heroin had risen from four to six.

Frequency of Drug Use

Respondents were asked if they had used drugs within the previous six months, and if so how often. Their pattern of responses is depicted in *Tables 33* and *34*.

The overwhelming majority of respondents who had used illicit drugs were not regular users.

As noted above, respondents were asked whether or not they would find it hard or inconvenient to go without a drug or drugs for one month. Four respondents reported that they would have serious difficulty and five stated that they would experience mild inconvenience from such abstinence.

Discussion

Over a quarter of the study group reported having at some time used illicit drugs. Overwhelmingly, such use was limited and was mainly confined to cannabis and amphetamines.

Table 33 Frequency of illicit drug use within previous six months amongst males (n = 436)

drug	less than once per month		at least once monthly		frequency 1–3 times per week		4–6 times per week		every day		total during past six months	
	n	%	n	%	n	%	n	%	n	%	n	%
cannabis	39	9.0	14	3.2	17	3.9	2	0.5	6	1.4	78	17.9
LSD	8	1.8	2	0.5	2	0.5	0	—	0	—	12	2.7
barbiturates	2	0.5	0	—	0	—	0	—	0	—	0	—
Mogadon	1	0.2	0	—	0	—	0	—	0	—	0	—
Librium	0	—	0	—	0	—	0	—	0	—	0	—
Valium	5	1.1	1	0.2	1	0.2	0	—	0	—	7	1.6
glues/solvents	1	0.2	2	0.5	0	—	0	—	0	—	3	0.7
amphetamines	13	3.0	4	0.9	2	0.5	0	—	0	—	19	4.4
opium	1	0.2	1	0.2	0	—	0	—	0	—	2	0.5
morphine	1	0.2	0	—	0	—	0	—	0	—	1	0.2
heroin	2	0.5	0	—	0	—	0	—	0	—	2	0.5
Methadone	1	0.2	—	—	—	—	—	—	—	—	1	0.2
cocaine	4	0.9	1	0.2	0	—	0	—	0	—	5	1.1
sleeping-tablets/tranquillizers	2	0.5	1	0.2	0	—	0	—	0	—	3	0.7
hallucinogenic fungi	6	1.4	0	—	1	0.2	0	—	0	—	1	0.2

Table 34 Frequency of illicit drug use within previous six months amongst females (n = 514)

drug	less than once per month		at least once monthly		frequency 1–3 times per week		4–6 times per week		every day		total during past six months	
	n	%	n	%	n	%	n	%	n	%	n	%
cannabis	41	8.0	16	3.1	9	1.7	0	—	1	0.2	67	13.0
LSD	2	0.4	2	0.4	0	—	0	—	0	—	4	0.8
barbiturates	2	0.4	0	—	0	—	0	—	0	—	2	0.4
Mogadon	2	0.4	0	—	0	—	0	—	0	—	2	0.4
Librium	0	—	0	—	0	—	0	—	1	0.2	1	0.2
Valium	1	0.2	0	—	0	—	0	—	2	0.4	3	0.6
glues/solvents	1	0.2	0	—	1	0.2	0	—	0	—	2	0.4
amphetamines	13	2.5	2	0.4	1	0.2	1	0.2	0	—	17	3.3
opium	0	—	0	—	0	—	0	—	0	—	0	—
morphine	0	—	0	—	0	—	0	—	0	—	0	—
heroin	2	0.4	0	—	0	—	0	—	0	—	2	0.4
cocaine	5	1.0	0	—	0	—	0	—	0	—	5	1.0
sleeping-tablets/tranquillizers	3	0.6	0	—	0	—	0	—	1	0.2	4	0.8
hallucinogenic fungi	4	0.8	0	—	0	—	0	—	0	—	4	0.8

As shown by *Table 32* there had been a great increase in the level of self-reported drug experience of the study group between 1979/80 and 1983. In fact this may be an effect of older people having more chance to experiment. It is also due to the increase in the availability of illicit drugs during the study period. This was widely reported by the police, social workers, clinicians, and others in contact with young illicit drug users (Advisory Council on the Misuse of Drugs 1982). In addition both drug seizures by customs and police and the number of 'addicts' notified to the Home Office increased considerably, as noted in Chapter 1. Some newspaper reports alleged that in certain areas of Britain a very high proportion of young people were using opiates, and that drug dependence was widespread. In fact such reports appeared to be largely speculative since there are few 'hard facts' with which to substantiate any form of prevalence estimates. In addition at least some of the tabloid newspaper coverage has suggested that opiate use in itself is synonymous with drug dependence or implies that the user is a 'problem drug taker'.

The results of the present study do not form a basis for generalization to young people in other areas. It is certain that illicit drug use varies from one place to another.

Very few drug surveys have been conducted in Britain since the mid-1970s. Most of those conducted earlier were confined to specific areas or to atypical subgroups of people such as students. One such study collected questionnaire information from secondary (high) school pupils in Wolverhampton in 1969, 1974, and 1979. The researchers concluded that: 'Contact with drugs and drug-taking increased over the first five years, but this trend was not continued through to 1979. Television remained the most important source of information about drugs, while peer groups and social pressures remained the most important reasons for starting to take drugs' (Wright and Pearl 1981: 793).

During January, 1982, NOP Market Research Ltd conducted a survey of a representative sample of 1,326 people aged 15–21 in 101 British parliamentary constituencies. This revealed that 29 per cent of respondents in Scotland reported having used illicit drugs. Nine per cent reported having used either heroin or cocaine. The overall pattern of responses to this survey is shown in *Table 35*.

As *Table 35* indicates, the level of cannabis use in Scotland was higher than anywhere else except London. In addition, levels of bar-biturate, LSD, heroin, and cocaine use reported in Scotland were also above those reported in England and Wales. This survey included a

Table 35 Regional variations in self-reported illicit drug use amongst the 15–21 age group in Britain

drugs ever used (n = 57★)	Scotland (n = 447★)	north of England (n = 338★)	Midlands, East Anglia, Wales (n = 330★)	south of England excluding London (n = 153★)	London
	%	%	%	%	%
cannabis	21	15	16	13	28
amphetamines	8	4	6	3	10
glues	2	5	1	2	4
barbiturates	16	2	4	2	3
LSD	8	3	4	2	3
heroin	7	★★	1	1	1
cocaine	9	1	1	1	3

★weighted total
★★less than 0.5%
(Source: NOP Market Research Ltd 1982)

very small Scottish sample. Even so, it does suggest that drug use is by no means uniform across Britain. This is consistent with evidence showing that officially recorded rates of tobacco- and alcohol-related problems are also highly variable in different areas (Plant 1981a).

A second study, the British Crime Survey, was conducted during 1981 and produced some relevant information. This included data collected by interview with people aged 16 and above in 5,031 households in central and southern Scotland. Three per cent of those interviewed in this survey reported that they had, at some time, smoked cannabis (Mott 1985). The same survey showed that 19 per cent of Scottish respondents aged 20–24 had at some time used cannabis, compared with 16 per cent of their counterparts in England and Wales.

Levels of youthful illicit drug use appear to vary considerably between different countries. Two recent publications have compared levels of self-reported drug use in Canada, India, Malaysia, Mexico, and Pakistan (Smart, Mora, Terroba, and Varma 1981; Smart, Arif, Hughes, Mora, Navaratnam, Varma, and Wadud 1981). These showed that amongst samples of people in their teens and early twenties (variously defined) the percentage of those having used illicit substances ranged from 5.9 per cent (in India) to 91.9 per cent (in

Pakistan). In Toronto 65.8 per cent of a sample of people aged 14–25 had used some form of illicit drug. Cannabis was by far the most widely used substance, having been taken by 63 per cent of non-students and 43.2 per cent of students. Three per cent of the Canadian non-students and 7 per cent of students had used opiates. Elsewhere levels of opiate use were much higher. Nearly a quarter of Mexican students and 14.5 per cent of non-students had used such drugs. Opiate use (in the form of opium) was also reported by 3.6 per cent of young people in India and 13.1 per cent in Pakistan. Daily drug use (except in Pakistan where it was reported by 71.1 per cent) was reported by only a tiny minority, ranging from 0.3 per cent to 2.1 per cent.

Fishburne, Abelson, and Cisin (1980) reported that in 1979, 69 per cent of those aged 18–21 surveyed in the United States had at some time used cannabis; this proportion had increased steadily from 40 per cent in 1971. Other American studies reviewed by Kandel (1982) confirm that levels of drug use in the United States are much higher than amongst respondents in the present study.

> 'Prevalence of use differs markedly for various drugs, with legal drugs (legal for adults, that is) being used much more frequently than illegal ones. Amongst the illicit drugs, use of marijuana is most prevalent. Thus in the 1981 national cohort of high school seniors, lifetime prevalence was 93 per cent for alcohol, 71 per cent for smoking and 60 per cent for marijuana. The proportions having ever used any of the other illicit drugs were much lower, ranging from 1 per cent for heroin.'
>
> (Kandel 1982: 330)

The levels of drug use reported in the present study were by no means exceptional by international standards, even though they are higher than those noted in several earlier British studies (Stimson 1981).

An extra word of caution is warranted in relation to survey information about illicit drugs. It is acknowledged that surveys of drinking habits are frequently beset by considerable underreporting (e.g. Pernanen 1974; Midanik 1982a). Information about illicit drug use is probably no less, and possibly far more, biased. Accordingly the results of surveys such as the present study need to be interpreted with caution and in the light of other available information. The NOP results were not widely different from those obtained by the present study. However, they do relate to a different age group and to a completely different geographical basis. Neither survey is discrepant with the assertion that in some areas there are 'pockets' of much more common opiate and other drug use. Even so, both surveys suggest that the general level of illicit drug use is markedly higher than that a decade earlier (Stimson 1981).

This conclusion may alarm many readers as further evidence of a sinister trend. It is emphasized, however, that the present study offers further confirmation that most illicit drug use is not regular and does not involve self-reported problems. Only a tiny minority of those who had used illicit drugs reported having experienced harm thereby or being daily drug users. These conclusions are quite conventional, but are worth emphasizing in view of the high level of public concern that youthful drug use provokes.

7 The Correlates of Alcohol, Tobacco, and Illicit Drug Use and Misuse

It is of some interest to examine how the use and misuse of alcohol, tobacco, and illicit drugs vary amongst different subgroups of respondents. Two subgroups are of particular interest. They are those from different social-class backgrounds and the unemployed.

SOCIAL CLASS

It has frequently been suggested that patterns of legal and illegal drug use may vary considerably between social classes (e.g. Dight 1976; Wilson 1980b; Royal College of Physicians 1983; Stimson 1981). Generally, this was not so in this study group. The following items were examined in relation to the social class of the head of the household in which each respondent was raised: alcohol consumption, experience of alcohol-related consequences, cigarette smoking and illicit drug use. In addition, separate consideration was given to the use of drugs such as LSD, cocaine, and heroin. These are included in Category A of the Misuse of Drugs Act 1971 and are hereafter referred to as 'Category A drugs'. Only one significant difference emerged from this procedure. Previous week's alcohol consumption was significantly higher amongst males from lower social-class backgrounds than amongst those from higher-class backgrounds. This is shown in *Table 36*.

The highest average level of alcohol consumption was reported by males from the Registrar General's social class III manual. Those from classes IV and V reported lower levels of consumption, and those from

Table 36 Previous week's alcohol consumption amongst respondents from different social class backgrounds

Registrar General's social class group	average previous week's alcohol consumption (units)	
	males	females
I professional/managerial	13.3	6.9
II intermediate non-manual	17.5	6.8
III skilled non-manual	20.1	5.5
III skilled manual	24.9	7.1
IV partly skilled manual	20.6	6.6
V unskilled manual	21.4	4.8

class I and II backgrounds reported the lowest levels of all. Social-class differences amongst females were not significant. Even so, those in the social class III manual group were also the heaviest drinkers, though only marginally so. For both sexes social class was not associated with the total number of alcohol-related consequences reportedly experienced. Overall patterns of alcohol, tobacco, and drug use and misuse were not linked to social class. In addition specific types of drug use, such as cannabis or amphetamine use, did not vary in relation to social class.

EMPLOYMENT AND UNEMPLOYMENT

The previous week's alcohol consumption of respondents who were currently in different work/educational settings was examined. The pattern that emerged is shown in *Table 37*.

Significant differences were evident amongst males but not amongst females. Even so, amongst both sexes those in full-time work were drinking much the same as those who were unemployed and seeking work. A curious subgroup of three males reported heavy alcohol consumption. These were all currently on the government's Youth Opportunities Programme, a scheme for young unemployed people. These reported a mean previous week's alcohol consumption of 70.3 units, the equivalent of roughly 35 pints of beer or two bottles of spirits.

Twelve per cent of the study group were unemployed at the time of their interviews during 1983. These were compared with other

Table 37 Previous week's alcohol consumption amongst respondents in different work or educational settings

current work/educational setting	average alcohol consumption in units	
	males (n = 433)	females (n = 496)
full-time employment	21.6 (n = 244)	6.8 (n = 296)
part-time employment	11.2 (n = 9)	11.5 (n = 13)
full-time education	15.6 (n = 106)	6.0 (n = 122)
unemployed and seeking work	23.2 (n = 55)	8.0 (n = 41)
unemployed and not seeking work	18.2 (n = 6)	5.0 (n = 1)
Youth Opportunities Programme	70.3 (n = 3)	3.4 (n = 7)
housewife/mother	—	2.1 (n = 10)
other	22.9 (n = 10)	3.5 (n = 6)

respondents in relation to alcohol, tobacco, and illicit drug use. As already noted, there were no significant differences between the unemployed and other respondents in relation to previous week's alcohol consumption. Consistent with this, tobacco smoking did not differ between the two subgroups, either amongst males or amongst females. In marked contrast, levels of illicit drug use were much higher amongst both males and females who were unemployed than amongst their peers who were working or who were full-time students.

Table 38 Use of illicit drugs amongst respondents in different work or educational settings

current work/educational setting	average number of illicit drugs ever used	
	males (n = 431)	females (n = 505)
full-time employment	0.5 (n = 242)	0.3 (n = 299)
part-time employment	1.2 (n = 9)	1.0 (n = 15)
full-time education	0.5 (n = 107)	0.5 (n = 123)
unemployed and seeking work	1.4 (n = 54)	1.0 (n = 42)
unemployed and not seeking work	2.8 (n = 6)	2.3 (n = 3)
Youth Opportunities Programme	2.0 (n = 3)	0.3 (n = 7)
housewife/mother	—	1.2 (n = 10)
other	2.6 (n = 10)	0.3 (n = 6)

The considerable differences in levels of self-reported drug use between the unemployed and employed are indicated by *Table 38*.

Amongst both sexes, significant differences between the levels of drug use were reported by those in different work or educational settings. The highest levels of drug use were reported by those who were not working and in particular by those who were not seeking work. In addition, as shown by *Table 38*, a group of ten males whose employment was not classified also reported a high level of drug experience. Approximately one-fifth of those of either sex who were unemployed had used three or more types of illicit drugs compared with only 5 or 6 per cent of those who were not unemployed.

The past (1979/80) psychoactive drug use and misuse of unemployed and employed respondents was examined in order to ascertain whether such factors were associated with subsequent unemployment. Five variables were considered. These were previous week's alcohol consumption, alcohol-related consequences, serious alcohol-related consequences, tobacco smoking, and illicit drug use. Amongst males, only tobacco smoking differed significantly but weakly during 1979/80 between respondents who were later unemployed and those who were not. Amongst females, previous week's alcohol consumption and illicit drug use were weakly predictive of unemployment. It is not suggested that much importance can be placed upon these conclusions. The link between drinking, smoking, or illicit drug use in 1979/80 and unemployment during 1983 is weak, obscure, and probably irrelevant. By themselves these very modest associations are of trivial importance. They cast little light upon the many possible factors associated with youth unemployment. One conclusion may be drawn: respondents who were unemployed during 1983 were not initially strikingly, or in most respects even slightly, more 'drug-oriented' than were those who were not unemployed. In other words, the alcohol, tobacco, and illicit drug use of the study group was not clearly related to later unemployment. In addition alcohol-related consequences and serious consequences were quite unrelated to subsequent unemployment. To reiterate, the comparison of job status with earlier psychoactive drug use failed to identify a distinctive subgroup of 'substance-oriented' young people who were subsequently found to experience high levels of unemployment. This conclusion is in marked contrast to the much higher levels of drug use that were evident amongst unemployed respondents during 1983.

A total of 454 respondents reported having been unemployed at some time since leaving school. The relationship between psychoactive drug use during 1979/80 and subsequent duration of unemployment was examined. As shown by *Table 39*, only a few weak associations emerged from this analysis.

As *Table 39* indicates, duration of unemployment amongst females was not significantly associated with either alcohol consumption or alcohol-related consequences as measured during 1979/80. Amongst males, however, both alcohol consumption on last drinking occasion

Table 39   Correlations between duration of unemployment since leaving school and previous psychoactive drug use and misuse

'predictive' variables measured in 1979/80	males (n = 189)	females (n = 172)
alcohol consumption during last drinking occasion	+0.1*	NS
number of cigarettes smoked daily	NS	+0.1*
number of illicit drugs ever used	NS	+0.1*
number of alcohol-related consequences experienced	NS	NS
number of serious alcohol-related consequences experienced	+0.2*	NS

NS not significant
*significant

and the number of serious alcohol-related consequences were significantly, though very weakly, associated with duration of subsequent unemployment. It is also evident that cigarette and illicit drug use amongst males was unrelated to duration of unemployment. The converse was again true for females, but these correlations (+0.13 and +0.15 respectively) were once more extremely small.

These results, like those related to current unemployment and previous psychoactive drug use, need to be interpreted with caution. Once more they indicate rather different things for males and females. Only a very tenuous level of association emerged between previous psychoactive drug use and duration of unemployment. Once more these results do not show a distinctive subgroup of young people whose 'deviant' drug use was succeeded by high levels of unemployment. This conclusion is reinforced since the results noted in the previous paragraph were obtained after controlling for two of the most important likely influences on youthful unemployment, social class and educational qualifications.

It is emphasized that only very limited conclusions may justifiably be drawn from this brief examination of the association between unemployment with current or earlier use of alcohol, tobacco, and illicit drugs.

ALCOHOL, TOBACCO, AND ILLICIT DRUG USE AND MISUSE

In Chapter 3 it was noted that general patterns of alcohol use and misuse in the first phase of the study were positively correlated with both tobacco and illicit drug use. A similar finding emerged from the 1983 interview data. The levels of association noted between the main measures of substance use are shown in *Tables 40* and *41*.

Amongst both sexes alcohol use and misuse were significantly and positively correlated with both tobacco and illicit drug use. Amongst both males and females illicit drug use was more strongly associated

Table 40 Correlations between alcohol, tobacco, and illicit drug use and misuse (males)

	previous week's alcohol consumption	no. of alcohol-related consequences experienced	no. of serious alcohol-related consequences experienced	no. of cigarettes smoked daily	no. of illicit drugs ever used
number of alcohol-related consequences experienced	+0.5★				
number of serious alcohol-related consequences experienced	+0.4★	+0.8★			
number of cigarettes smoked daily	+0.3★	+0.2★	+0.2★		
number of illicit drugs ever used	+0.5★	+0.4★	+0.3★	+0.3★	
number of Category A drugs ever used	+0.4★	+0.2★	+0.2★	+0.2★	+0.7★

★ significant

Table 41 Correlations between alcohol, tobacco, and illicit drug use and misuse (females)

	previous week's alcohol consumption	no. of alcohol- related consequences experienced	no. of serious alcohol- related consequences experienced	no. of cigarettes smoked daily	no. of illicit drugs ever used
number of alcohol- related consequences experienced	+0.4*				
number of serious alcohol-related consequences experienced	+0.3*	+0.8*			
number of cigarettes smoked daily	+0.3*	+0.3*	+0.3*		
number of illicit drugs ever used	+0.5*	+0.6*	+0.6*	+0.3*	
number of Category A drugs ever used	+0.4*	+0.4*	+0.3*	+0.2*	+0.7*

* significant

with alcohol use and experience of alcohol-related consequences than was cigarette smoking. These results reinforce the conclusion noted, both in Chapter 3 and in many other studies, that a young heavy drinker was quite likely also to be 'a man (or woman) of substance', more commonly described as a polydrug user.

Discussion

Social Class

The only significant association to emerge between social class and alcohol, tobacco, and illicit drug use and misuse related to alcohol consumption amongst males. As noted above, those from higher-class backgrounds reported drinking significantly less than did those from lower-class homes. This result is consistent with that obtained by many other studies (e.g. Cahalan, Cisin, and Crossley 1969; Edwards, Chandler, and Hensman 1972; Dight 1976; Wilson 1980b). The lack of a corresponding significant difference amongst females is not an unusual finding. As shown by *Table 36* alcohol consumption amongst females did differ slightly by social class. These results were not very different from those for women, obtained by Dight (1976). Amongst 'regular drinkers' (those who had drunk in the previous week) Dight had found very small social-class differences amongst young women. Amongst men aged 17–30 Dight found that those in social class III drank the least. This is in marked contrast to the conclusions in the present study that this group drank most of all. Even so, this difference may be attributable to the fact that Dight's results related to a much wider age range than did the results of the present study.

The 1978 survey conducted by Wilson (1980b) produced broadly but not completely similar results to those shown in *Table 36*. Wilson concluded: 'In Scotland, men from non-manual occupations consistently drank less than those in manual occupations. . . . Women in middle-class households drank slightly more than those from working-class households both in England and Wales and Scotland' (Wilson 1980b: 16).

As *Table 36* shows, Wilson's results were echoed by those of the present study for males but not for females. Amongst the latter the highest level of alcohol consumption was reported by those from skilled manual backgrounds, although this difference was not significant. Like Dight's, however, Wilson's results referred to a much older age group and are not strictly comparable to this study.

A recent survey of adolescent drinking in America indicated that:

'there are small but real differences between families in which the main wage earner is in a blue collar occupation and those in which he is in a white collar occupation; teenagers from blue collar backgrounds are a bit more likely to be non-drinkers (this is also true when the data are broken down by sex).'

(Zucker and Harford 1983: 977)

In Chapter 3 it was noted that the overall substance use of the study group did not differ significantly according to whether or not respondents came from manual (blue-collar) backgrounds. This is reaffirmed for females and for males except in relation to the alcohol consumption of the latter.

Employment and Unemployment

The relationship between alcohol use and unemployment has been widely discussed and available evidence is contradictory (e.g. Brenner

1979; Plant 1979a; Kilich and Plant 1981; Kendell, de Roumanie, and Ritson 1983; Fagin and Little 1984). In more general terms it appears that the use and misuse of both alcohol and illicit drugs increase when the 'real' costs of those commodities are lowest. As noted by Smart and Murray: 'alcohol consumption decreases during economic depressions' (1983: 298).

Extreme caution needs to be exercised in the interpretation of evidence on general trends in the economy and health trends. As forcefully noted by Kasl: 'ecological analysis leads to results which, *by themselves*, are opaque, unhelpful, potentially misleading' (1979: 785).

The results of this study suggest that unemployment was indeed unrelated to the use of alcohol but was associated with high levels of illicit drug use. These levels were striking and are subject to many possible interpretations. The most parsimonious explanation is that unemployment, in some way yet to be determined, leads to greater drug use. Another explanation, which is not necessarily mutually exclusive, is that illicit drugs may have been relatively attractive to unemployed young people because the 'real costs' of such substances have been declining in relation to those of alcohol and tobacco (Ashton 1984). Other interpretations include the often noted possibility that unemployed young people, having little stake in the 'workaday world', find the drug scene, or at least drug experimentation, more appealing than do their working peers (e.g. Young 1971; Plant 1975). These interpretations, though plausible, are speculative. Nevertheless it has been noted that some young people in the United Kingdom do now choose between legal and illicit drugs on the basis of their respective costs (Rorstad 1984). It has also been suggested by Thorley (1983) that there may be some form of 'hydraulic' relationship between legal and illicit drugs, so that one substance may be used as a substitute for another, depending upon price and availability. Many factors may account for the high rate of drug experience amongst the unemployed people in this study. This issue might only be resolved by much more thorough interviews either with these respondents or with other unemployed young people. The possible willingness of some people to substitute illicit for legal drugs must be considered in the formulation of alcohol-control policies. It must be noted that opiates have, in the past, been used as substitutes for alcohol. Berridge and Edwards (1981), reviewing opium use in nineteenth-century Britain, concluded: 'The belief was that working people were turning to opium for "non-medical" or "stimulant" purposes, that their use was not for medical reasons at all, but that they used the drug as a cheaper alternative to drink' (1981: 106).

CONCLUSION

The association between alcohol, tobacco, and illicit drugs has already been discussed in relation to the information collected during 1979 and 1980. The interview data collected during 1983 produced support for the original conclusion about the significant relationship between different types of psychoactive drug use. As shown by *Tables 40* and *41* alcohol consumption and experience of alcohol-related consequences, cigarette smoking, and illicit drug use were all intercorrelated both amongst males and females. Moreover, for both sexes higher levels of correlation emerged between alcohol use and misuse and illicit drug use than between cigarette smoking and illicit drug use. Dight (1976) had discovered that tobacco use was the best correlate of illicit drug use. The present results show that amongst this particular group of young people illicit drug experimentation was even more strongly related to alcohol use and the experience of alcohol-related consequences than was tobacco smoking. As already noted, the overwhelming majority of drugs used by the study group had been used only rarely or infrequently. Very few of those interviewed appeared to be frequent users of illicit drugs. These results reinforce those described in many other studies (e.g. Wechsler and Rohman 1981) according to which illicit drug experimentation, though clearly different in important respects from alcohol use, lies along the same continuum. This appears to be the case for the females as much as for males in this study.

8 The Predictors of Alcohol, Tobacco, and Illicit Drug Use and Misuse

The primary aim of this study was: 'To determine whether the knowledge, attitudes, and behaviour concerning alcohol among school-leavers predict subsequent alcohol-related behaviour.'

In order to resolve this issue, responses to the first phase of the study in 1979/80 were compared to those elicited in the third phase during 1983. A very wide range of factors was included in this comparison, for example baseline measures of alcohol, tobacco, and illicit drug use and misuse, biographical details, and attitudes. These were related not only to the use and misuse of alcohol reported in 1983, but also to patterns of tobacco and illicit drug use. Only very low levels of association were obtained from this procedure. These are not described in detail. *Table 42* shows the correlations that emerged between alcohol, tobacco, and illicit drug use and misuse.

The alcohol consumption and alcohol-related consequences of respondents during 1979/80 were poor predictors of these variables during 1983. Alcohol consumption during 1979/80 was, at best, only very weakly correlated with that four years later. Alcohol-related consequences reported during 1979/80 were not even slightly predictive of those reported in 1983. Amongst females, the reverse was evident. Consequences reported during 1979/80 were (just) predictive of later consequences.

For both sexes tobacco smoking and illicit drug use were more highly predictive of the same behaviour four years later. This is presumably because tobacco use far more often involves physical dependence, and illicit drug use, by definition, is a fairly 'deviant' activity. In contrast, most drinking is not illicit nor does it involve physical dependence.

Table 42 Correlations between patterns of alcohol, tobacco, and illicit druguse and misuse in 1979/80 and during 1983

variable	males	females
alcohol consumption on last occasion	+0.1 NS	0.2*
previous week's alcohol consumption	+0.2 *	−0.0 NS
number of alcohol-related consequences experienced	+0.0 NS	+0.1 *
tobacco smoking	+0.6 *	+0.6 *
illicit drugs**	+0.4 *	+0.3 *

NS not significant
* significant
** 1979/80 drug use was correlated with drugs used within 6 months of 1983 reinterview

The correlations obtained by comparing the 1979/80 and 1983 results are low. These results are not surprising. A number of authors (e.g. Peterson 1968; Mischel 1969) have pointed out that human behaviour is typically characterized by inconsistency across both place and time. Correlations of the level of +0.3 or less are commonplace and attitudes are not usually accurate guides to behaviour, except in special circumstances. To quote Mischel, there is: 'impressive evidence that on virtually all our dispositional measures of personality, substantial changes occur in the characteristics of the individual, longitudinally over time and even more dramatically across seemingly similar settings' (Mischel 1969: 1012).

There is little evidence that people behave in similar ways in different settings or at different times. It could therefore be expected that behaviour in relation to alcohol and other drugs should be similarly subject to inconsistency.

There are, however, circumstances when a greater degree of consistency is often observed, for example, extreme behaviour such as that found amongst people with serious psychiatric conditions, or individuals scoring at an extreme end of a behavioural rating. Thus Endler (1973) found that anxiety proneness was more consistent amongst neurotic patients than amongst 'normals'. Psychotics were more consistent than either.

In relation to the present study group, this raised the prospect that there might be a higher level of consistency amongst respondents whose alcohol and other drug use were atypically high during 1979/80. This possibility was investigated separately for each sex. A subgroup of respondents was distinguished in relation to their self-reported alcohol consumption, serious alcohol-related problems, and illicit drug use during 1979/80. For each of these three factors, respondents were selected who were the highest-scoring 5 per cent (approximately) at the ages of 15 and 16. These high scorers were then examined in relation to their alcohol consumption and serious alcohol-related consequences, and illicit drug use at the ages of 19 and 20.

HIGH-SCORING RESPONDENTS

'Heavy' alcohol consumption (over 45 units in the previous week) in 1979/80 was not related to heavy alcohol consumption (over 50 units in the previous week) or serious alcohol-related consequences (as defined in Chapter 5) during 1983. Even so, it was predictive of illicit drug use at the age of 19 or 20. Amongst males who had been heavy drinkers at the age of 15 or 16, 81 per cent had used at least one illicit drug by the age of 19 or 20. However, of the moderate and light drinkers only 47 per cent reported having tried illicit drugs by the same age. Similarly, heavy-drinking 15- or 16-year-old males were also more likely to have used Category A drugs by the time they were 19 or 20 than were other males (19 per cent and 5 per cent respectively). Thus heavy drinking at the age of 15 or 16 was significantly associated with later illicit drug use, but not with later alcohol consumption nor with serious alcohol-related consequences.

Males were also divided between those who had and those who had not reported having two or more serious alcohol-related consequences (as defined in Chapter 3). High scorers were not more likely than low scorers to have become heavy drinkers, to have serious alcohol-related consequences (as defined in Chapter 5), or to have used illicit drugs or Category A drugs. Thus, experience of serious alcohol-related consequences was not predictive of heavy or 'problematic' substance use four years later.

Finally, males were divided between those who had and those who had not used illicit drugs at the age of 15 or 16. Those who had were more likely to be heavy drinkers (32 per cent versus 19 per cent), were more likely to have used at least two illicit drugs (29 per cent versus 16 per cent), and were also more likely to have taken drugs such as LSD (which are classified under Category A of the Misuse of Drugs Act) by 1983 (19 per cent versus 3 per cent). The relationship between cannabis use at the ages of 15 and 16 and later Category A drug use was also examined. A highly significant relationship emerged. No fewer than 36 per cent of cannabis users had later tried Category A drugs, compared with only 4 per cent of the other males. Drug use at the age of 15 or 16 did not predict later serious alcohol-related problems.

As they are less heavy drinkers than their male counterparts, the criterion for 15- and 16-year-old female 'heavy drinkers' was reduced to consumption of over 16 units in the previous week. Heavy-drinking females were not more likely to be heavy drinkers at the age of 19 or 20, nor were they more likely than others to have developed serious alcohol-related consequences (as defined in Chapter 5). In spite of this, female heavy drinkers at the age of 15 or 16 were significantly more likely to have used illicit drugs, but not Category A drugs.

Females who had experienced two or more serious alcohol-related consequences (as defined in Chapter 3) during 1979/80 were not more likely to be heavy drinkers by 1983. They had, however, experienced more serious alcohol-related consequences (33 per cent versus 9 per cent) (as defined in Chapter 5) and were more likely than other females to have tried at least one Category A drug (16 per cent versus 3 per cent). The general level of illicit drug use by 1983 was not predicted by earlier alcohol-related consequences.

Females who had used illicit drugs at the age of 15 or 16 were generally more likely to be heavy drinkers (13 per cent versus 1 per cent) and were more likely to have had two or more serious alcohol-related consequences (as defined in Chapter 5) (16 per cent versus 9 per cent). They were also more likely to have used at least two illicit drugs (24 per cent versus 6 per cent) and to have used Category A drugs (8 per cent versus 2 per cent).

As with males, there was a significant relationship between having used cannabis at the age of 15 or 16 and having used at least one Category A drug by 1983: of those who had used cannabis, 21 per cent had tried at least one Category A drug four years later compared with only 2 per cent of those who had not.

It would appear that there is little evidence of consistency in alcohol and drug use between 1979/80 and 1983. As the two preceding sections have shown, this consistency is rather greater when 'high scorers' are considered as a separate subgroup. This raised the possibility that amidst the shifting sands of varying 'normal' alcohol and drug use a hard core of extreme and problem users may have been hidden. This does not appear to be the case from this investigation. Five males were high scorers on alcohol consumption, serious alcohol-related consequences, and illicit drug use at the age of 15 or 16. Only two of these remained heavy drinkers and drug users by 1983.

Five females were also high scorers on alcohol consumption, serious alcohol-related consequences, and illicit drug use at the age of 15 or 16. None of these was a heavy drinker four years later and only one had used more types of illicit drugs.

In sum, only two of the males, but none of the females, were 'high scorers' on all three measures during both 1979/80 and 1983. These were, therefore, people who were consistently heavy users of alcohol and of illicit drugs, and who had consistently experienced serious alcohol-related consequences. In the present study group their number was very small. This is not, of course, to underestimate the seriousness of the position for the individuals (and families) involved.

UPBRINGING

The literature on alcohol and drug misuse contains many references to the importance of family background. Accordingly an examination was made of whether or not self-reported alcohol consumption varied in relation to upbringing. The results of this analysis are shown in *Table 43*.

No significance emerged amongst females. There was, however, a significant difference amongst males in respect of the alcohol con-

Table 43 Previous week's alcohol consumption in relation to upbringing

by whom respondent was brought up	average alcohol consumption in units (all respondents)	
	males (n = 433)	females (n = 496)
mother and father	19.35 (n = 338)	6.70 (n = 429)
mother only	29.00 (n = 13)	5.6 (n = 32)
father only	46.83 (n = 6)	8.00 (n = 5)
mother and stepfather	24.00 (n = 1)	5.22 (n = 9)
father and stepmother	— —	1.00 (n = 2)
grandparent(s)	0.00 (n = 1)	1.00 (n = 2)
fosterparents	— —	0.00 (n = 1)
other	28.00 (n = 24)	8.76 (n = 17)

sumption of those with different upbringing. As shown by *Table 43* the subgroup with the heaviest previous week's consumption comprised those (n=6) who had been raised only by their fathers. Males who had been raised by their mothers alone also reported a higher previous week's consumption than did those who had been raised by both parents.

Upbringing was also examined in relation to experience of alcohol-related consequences. Amongst both sexes significant differences emerged. These are shown in *Table 44*.

Table 44 Alcohol-related consequences in relation to upbringing

by whom respondent was brought up	mean alcohol-related consequences score	
	males (n = 437)	females (n = 509)
mother and father	5.3 (n = 392)	2.9 (n = 440)
mother only	8.2 (n = 13)	3.0 (n = 33)
father only	9.8 (n = 6)	7.6 (n = 5)
mother and stepfather	12.0 (n = 1)	3.0 (n = 9)
father and stepmother	—	3.0 (n = 1)
grandparent(s)	7.0 (n = 1)	1.0 (n = 2)
fosterparents	—	1.0 (n = 1)
other	5.5 (n = 24)	5.1 (n = 18)

The mean level of alcohol-related consequences amongst both males and females was higher amongst individuals who had been raised only by their father than amongst those who had been raised by both parents. In addition amongst males more consequences were also reported by those (n=13) who had been raised only by their mother or by their mother and stepfather (n=1).

Serious alcohol-related consequences were also significantly associated with upbringing for both sexes. Amongst both males and females those who had been raised only by their father reported significantly higher levels of such consequences than did those raised by both parents.

Significant differences also emerged for both sexes when respondents' upbringing was related to their cigarette use. Details of these differences are provided in *Tables 45* and *46*.

Amongst both males and females, those who had been brought up by single parents were more likely to smoke than were other respondents.

Table 45 Cigarette smoking and upbringing: males

number of cigarettes smoked daily	by whom respondent was brought up							
	n	%*	n	%*	n	%*	n	%
0	257	66.6	6	46.2	1	16.7	15	57.7
1 or less	16	4.1	1	7.7	—		—	
2–4	10	2.6	1	7.7	—		—	
5–10	31	8.0	1	7.7	1	16.7	4	15.4
11–20	60	15.5	4	30.8	2	33.3	6	23.1
21 or more	12	3.1	—		2	33.3	1	3.8
total	386	99.9	13	100.1	6	100.0	26	100.0

*calculated to nearest decimal place

The few individuals who had been raised solely by their father were even more likely to smoke than were those raised solely by their mother. One possible reason for this is that many young people may be influenced by their parents' smoking habits. Fathers were more likely to smoke than mothers.

Upbringing was examined in relation to the use of drugs included in Category A of the Misuse of Drugs Act, 1971. These include heroin, LSD, and cocaine. Amongst both males and females, no overall sig-

Table 46 Cigarette smoking and upbringing: females

number of cigarettes smoked daily	by whom respondent was brought up							
	mother & father		mother only		father only		other	
	n	%*	n	%*	n	%*	n	%
0	277	63.7	17	53.1	1	20.0	10	32.2
1 or less	29	6.7	—		—		4	12.9
2–4	14	3.2	1	3.1	1	20.0	—	
5–10	44	10.1	7	21.9	—	—	3	9.7
11–20	64	14.7	6	18.8	3	60.0	11	35.5
21 or more	7	1.6	1	3.1	—		3	9.7
total	435	100.0	32	100.0	5	100.0	31	100.0

*calculated to nearest decimal point

nificant differences emerged in this respect. Similarly no significant differences emerged when the relationship between upbringing and overall numbers of illicit drugs used was examined.

ALCOHOL EDUCATION

The second aim of this study related to the effectiveness of alcohol education. It was not known how elaborate or intensive had been any alcohol education to which respondents had been exposed at school. Approximately 50 per cent of the male respondents reported in 1979/80 that they had received information or had had lessons or discussions about alcohol and drinking whilst they were at school. Those who had received this health education were compared with those who had not, in terms of drinking, drug use, and experience of alcohol-related consequences four years later. The only significant difference was that boys who had received such education were significantly, but slightly, more likely to have used a greater range of illicit drugs than those males who had not received health education (mean of 0.9 drugs used, versus 0.6). Of those males who reported having been shown a film about alcohol at school (31 per cent), there was again a number of significant differences. Males who had seen such a film drank more alcohol four years later (mean of 26 units versus mean of 18 units), and were likely to have experienced more alcohol-related consequences (mean of 6.2 versus 5.1).

Females who had had alcohol education at school (52 per cent) were subsequently more likely than those who had not to experience serious alcohol-related consequences (mean of 0.7 versus 0.5). Similarly, females who reported having seen an alcohol education film at school (25 per cent) were also more likely to have experienced more serious alcohol-related consequences (mean 0.8 versus 0.5).

These associations are, of course, contrary to those desired and expected. On the surface they would appear to suggest that receiving alcohol education or seeing an alcohol education film are likely to be associated with higher levels of subsequent alcohol consumption and alcohol-related consequences, as well as with illicit drug experience. This is a puzzling finding which is difficult to explain. Even so the consistency of the results obtained suggests that this is a 'real' rather than a 'chance' finding. Although these results were significant they were of small magnitude.

DISCUSSION

Overall Levels of Prediction

It would appear that when the study group as a whole was examined there was little evidence of consistency in terms of alcohol, tobacco, and illicit drug use and misuse. Even when the extreme scorers were examined the degree of consistency was not much higher. Thus, for example, there was a significant tendency for 15- and 16-year-old females who had experienced two or more serious alcohol-related consequences to have used Category A drugs by the age of 19 or 20. Even so 84 per cent of those females did not do so. It is of interest to note the pattern of relationships with the extreme scorers. In particular, for both males and females, heavy drinking during 1979/80 was not related to heavy drinking during 1983. However, illicit drug use at the earlier age was related to subsequent heavy drinking. Similarly, for both sexes, heavy drinking at 15 or 16 was related to later illicit drug use. It would appear that at the age of 15 or 16 heavy alcohol consumption is a 'deviant behaviour' (as is the use of illicit drugs). Both of these behaviour patterns were associated with similar 'deviance' four years later. However, at 19 or 20 heavy drinking is not a particularly deviant behaviour pattern. Heavy alcohol use at 15 or 16 in both sexes is relatively unrelated to later alcohol-related consequences. Conversely, illicit drug use at the age of 15 or 16 was more strongly and significantly associated with heavy drinking, alcohol-related consequences, and further illicit drug use.

The results of this study clearly indicate that amongst this particular study group, patterns of self-reported alcohol, tobacco, and illicit drug use were far from static entities. In particular alcohol consumption during 1979/80 did not predict consumption four years later. This is consistent with Fillmore's (1974) results from a study of American college students. These indicated that there is widespread movement between harm-free and harmful drinking. In a second publication, Fillmore concluded that: 'Problems which tend to characterize young problem drinkers are not necessarily those which serve as good predictive tools for later problems' (Fillmore 1975: 903).

Fillmore's comments related to a twenty-year follow-up study of 206 respondents who were aged 16 to 25 when first interviewed as part of an initial study group of 17,000 college students. Her results indicated that: 'if a respondent drank in youth and reported alcohol problems, it could be predicted beyond the operation of chance that he or she would report problems 20 years later' (Fillmore 1975: 902).

In fact the intercorrelations obtained by Fillmore between her two waves of data were mainly fairly low and were similar to those obtained by a comparison between the first and third waves of the present study.

Donovan, Jessor, and Jessor (1983) have reported the results of a longitudinal study of adolescent psychosocial development conducted in the United States between 1972/73 and 1979. This study related to 595 young adults. The authors were brought to conclusions which are strikingly similar to those derived from the present study:

'With respect to the continuity – non continuity of problem drinking between adolescence or youth on one hand, and on young adulthood on the other, this pattern of drinking does not continue into young adulthood for the majority of the adolescent problem drinkers in our samples. . . . Most of the high-school adolescents and the college youth in our sample, then, appear to have "matured" of earlier involvement in problem drinking by their middle or late twenties.'

(Donovan, Jessor, and Jessor 1983: 131)

One of the more striking results of the present study was the fact that alcohol use during 1979/80 predicted illicit drug use four years later. Kandel (1982) has suggested that there is a sequence of youthful drug involvement which frequently leads from legal substances, such as alcohol and tobacco, to illicit drugs such as cannabis and opiates. She has noted:

'One of the most intriguing findings to emerge from longitudinal drug studies is that the antecedents of adolescent drug use appear to be similar in certain respects to those linked in other studies of adolescent psychopathology. . . . This question suggests that drug use and related behaviours in all likelihood cannot be properly studied apart from concurrent developmental processes in adolescence and in young adulthood. Involvement with drugs must be examined as one among several behavioural outcomes of psycho-social development processes' (Kandel 1982: 343).

The present study was largely concerned with youthful alcohol use and misuse. The results that have been produced add to an already considerable body of evidence that links the use or misuse of alcohol with that of tobacco and illicit drugs. This study collected a large amount of information, only some of which has been presented in this book. Even so, the authors share the view expressed by Kandel (1982) and by Donovan, Jessor, and Jessor (1983) that youthful alcohol and drug use can be fully understood only if future research also relates them to much broader issues and influences than those encompassed by the present investigation.

Upbringing

Patterns of alcohol and tobacco use were significantly associated with whether or not respondents had been raised by both of their parents. Illicit drug use, however, was not distinguished in this way. As already noted, the minority of male respondents who had not been raised by both parents were heavier drinkers and had experienced more alcohol-related consequences than had those who were raised by both parents. Amongst females, alcohol consumption was not significantly differentiated by upbringing yet significant differences were evident in relation to alcohol-related consequences.

Several earlier studies have concluded that alcohol misuse is frequently preceded by family disorganization or break-up (e.g. McCord and McCord 1962; Hassall 1968). Even so, this view is not unanimous. Hawker has concluded that: 'There was no evidence that young people from one parent families drank more or experienced more problems as a result of their drinking than those who lived with both parents' (Hawker 1978: 13).

It has been demonstrated by several studies that alcohol use amongst young people is influenced by the attitudes to alcohol and the drinking habits of parents (e.g. Jahoda and Crammond 1972; O'Connor 1978; Jessor and Jessor 1978). In addition Vaillant has recently noted:

'In 1940 Paul Schilder wrote "the chronic alcoholic person is one who from his earliest childhood on has lived in a state of insecurity". . . . Since then in virtually all retrospective studies of alcoholics (Barry 1974) and in the two best prospective studies (McCord and McCord 1960; Robins 1966) unstable childhood has seemed to predict future alcoholism. Broken homes, irresponsible fathers, marital discord, and inconsistent upbringing seem most often implicated.'

(Vaillant 1983a: 71)

It is interesting that although patterns of alcohol and tobacco use in the present study group were associated with family upbringing, illicit drug use was not. A recent review of aetiological theories of drug dependence concluded that family disturbance has been suggested as a contributory factor. This review also concluded:

'This impression changes when reference is made to control groups . . . Cockett (1971) and James and d'Orban (1970) found that the prevalence of such separation amongst institutionalized drug-takers they examined was no different from that amongst non-using but institutionalized comparison groups. The suggested link between drug misuse and parental separation becomes far less credible when users are compared with a control group.'

(Plant 1981b: 263)

The extensive literature on normal youthful drinking habits includes many suggestions that family background is influential, as well as several indications to the contrary. Smart, Gray, and Bennett (1978), commenting upon a survey of Ontario school pupils, noted that: 'Parental drinking and parental rejection and control have little unique explanatory power. It is suggested that parental modelling may be of most importance at the outset of drinking, whereas place and extent of drinking is most important in predicting the signs of heavy drinking' (Smart, Gray, and Bennett 1978: 1079–80).

Alcohol Education

This study provides some disturbing results in relation to the results of alcohol education. As noted above, at face value those who had received alcohol education or who had seen alcohol education films became heavier users and misusers of alcohol and illicit drugs than did those who had not. It is, of course, possible that 'substance-oriented' young people might be more likely to recall health education than those for whom alcohol and illicit drugs were less salient. There was no evidence, as indicated in Chapter 3, to suggest that those who had received alcohol education were heavier alcohol, tobacco, or illicit drug users than those who had not when first surveyed at the ages of 15 or 16. Even so, a number of other studies have concluded that health education in the alcohol, tobacco, and drug field has not produced dramatic results and that sometimes adverse effects have been produced. This is discussed in more detail in Chapter 9. It is emphasized that since so little was known about the type or adequacy of 'alcohol education' that had been encountered by half of the subjects of this study, very little may be concluded from these results by themselves. In spite of this, these findings are not very reassuring.

9 Conclusions and Discussion

This study was originally mounted to achieve two objectives. The first of these was to ascertain whether or not patterns of alcohol use and misuse amongst 15- and 16-year-olds predicted their drinking habits a few years later. The second aim related to assessing the effectiveness of alcohol education.

PREDICTING DRINKING HABITS

Drinking habits during 1979/80 were only a poor predictor of those during 1983. It had been hypothesized at the outset of this study that drinking habits at the age of 15 or 16 might serve to indicate such habits four years later. In fact they did not. Drinking habits amongst the study group were far more varied than had been anticipated, although such variation is consistent with that noted in several other studies. Only low correlations emerged between not only alcohol use and misuse, but also that of tobacco and illicit drugs when the 1979/80 and 1983 results were compared.

Even when attention was focused on respondents who had been 'heavy drinkers' in 1979/80 alcohol consumption did not serve as a predictor of subsequent drinking or alcohol-related consequences. This is probably the most important finding in relation to the primary aim of this study. It is, however, striking that heavy drinking during 1979/80 did predict later illicit drug experience.

Only amongst females did experience of alcohol-related consequences during 1979/80 serve to predict those reported during 1983. Amongst females initial alcohol-related consequences also predicted later illicit drug use.

Regarding illicit drug use during 1979/80 it emerged that this *did* predict later alcohol use as well as illicit drug experience. These results clearly justify the inclusion of illicit drug use in this study: drug use predicted later alcohol consumption, while alcohol consumption did not. This study did not identify a 'hard core' of young people who were the heaviest drinkers, smokers, and illicit drug users throughout this study period. Only two males fell into such a category and these were only a small minority of those who during 1983 were relatively heavy users of legal or illicit drugs.

These results reinforce earlier evidence that frequent heavy drinking is relatively commonplace amongst young people, but that their drinking habits often change. Blane has noted that: 'direct predictive relationships between young adults' frequent heavy drinking and middle aged alcoholic drinking are not strong' (Blane 1979: 30).

The present study, related only to a short follow-up of one group of youthful drinkers, supports a similar view in relation to the age range 15 and 16 to 19 and 20. As Blane has noted, 'frequent heavy drinking is a self-limiting condition' (Blane 1979: 32).

This conclusion corresponds closely to the results of this study. The implications of this are far from clear. It certainly appears that it is not worth while attempting to 'detect' or 'screen' for incipient alcohol dependence within the age range covered by this study since the overwhelming majority of those identified as being 'at risk' will probably not be in a few years' time. In addition the value of directing alcohol education at teenagers as some form of preventive strategy may be reduced by the fact that the future drinking habits of this group bear very little relation to their drinking while at school.

EVALUATING ALCOHOL EDUCATION

The initial results of this study indicated that half of the study group had received some form of alcohol education. Unfortunately none of the five schools included in this study provided alcohol education in a systematic or elaborate way. Accordingly it is far from clear what the alcohol education reportedly provided had consisted of, or when it was given. In consequence the results of this study cannot be regarded as a definitive evaluation of this education. In spite of this it is remarkable that self-reported experience of alcohol education or exposure to an alcohol education film was associated with significant (if small) increases in subsequent alcohol consumption, alcohol-related consequences, and illicit drug use. This finding, although clearly related to an uncertain entity, is not a reassuring one. To explain it one must enter the realms of pure speculation. It is emphasized that these strange results cannot be accepted as evidence that alcohol education *leads to* or *causes* heavy or harmful alcohol or illicit drug use.

Health education is an important aspect of several policy options in relation to the alcohol, tobacco, and illicit drug use of young people. It is discussed in more detail later in this chapter.

RESPONDING TO ALCOHOL, TOBACCO, AND ILLICIT DRUG
PROBLEMS

At the time of writing, alcohol consumption and misuse in the United Kingdom are at relatively high levels. These levels are rather lower than those at the beginning of the century and they have recently been declining due, amongst other things, to the effects of recession. Tobacco smoking in the United Kingdom has also been declining and the proportion of the population who smoke has dropped considerably during the past decade. Illicit drug use, however, appears to be increasing steadily.

Aetiology

The formulation of realistic policies to curb the misuse of psychoactive drugs should be influenced by evidence about what leads to such misuse. An extensive literature has been produced that has sought to explain the reasons for psychoactive substance use, misuse, and dependence. It has been suggested that if the cause or causes of drug misuse could be identified, then a solution might be devised. In fact the aetiology of drug use and misuse is a confusing subject. Several authors have concluded that many influences are relevant. Edwards has suggested that: 'Drug-related behaviour is the interaction between drug, personality and environment' (1974: 179).

Many aetiological theories have been advanced. Most of these are plausible, though they have to coexist with contradictory theories that are equally valid. The literature, for example on the role of personality factors, contains many contradictory results and conclusions. Plant recently concluded:

'The literature referring to aetiological factors of drug use and drug dependence is extensive and repetitive. Many separate theories exist and most of these are consistent with certain observed features of some sub-groups of drug users. As Fazey (1973) has concluded from her parallel review of aetiological factors, the literature as a whole has many weaknesses. There have been few studies of representative groups of drug-takers and most data have been related to highly atypical groups such as those in clinics or custodial institutions, whose presence in such institutions may have been influenced by many factors. Few studies have used control groups, so that excessive emphasis has been placed upon traits such as parental deprivation which may be as common amongst non-drug-takers as amongst drug-takers. Most studies have based their assumptions upon characteristics identified in established drug-takers. This has led to confusion between mere *correlates* and *causes* of drug use . . . . No narrow explanation seems capable of accounting for the range of data and theories. . . . Apart from the limitations of current aetiological research, it appears likely that different types of drug-related behaviour may have different causes. Initial drug use may depend upon social factors, such as peer pressure and availability. Progression to greater involvement or dependence may be attributable to different factors, such as personality abnormalities or social deprivation. In addition, a third set of factors may explain why some drug users remain dependent, while others do not. There are so many types of drug users and so many types of drug use that the profusion of different (yet largely compatible) theories, is hardly surprising.'

(Plant 1981a: 272–73)

Peck, considering the aetiology of alcohol use and misuse, drew similar conclusions:

'This review shows that a large number and wide range of determining factors have been identified in relation to alcohol abuse. *There is therefore no single cause.* In any individual, several factors are likely to be simultaneously operative; and in a second individual, a completely different set of factors may be important.'

(Peck 1982: 82)

These conclusions about the aetiology of drug use, misuse, and dependence are crucial to the design and execution of policies to curb alcohol, tobacco, and drug-related problems. A comprehensive review of such strategies is beyond the scope of this book. In spite of this it is appropriate to discuss some policy options, with particular reference to health education. It is emphasized that while some alcohol, tobacco, and drug problems (and in consequence some control policies) are particularly relevant to young people, many are not. It would be quite unrealistic to attempt to curb youthful alcohol, tobacco, or drug use and misuse in isolation from policies designed to limit and regulate those of the general population.

Controlling Availability

There is a clear relationship between the availability of alcohol, tobacco, and illicit drugs and their levels of use and misuse. As noted in Chapter 1, the post-war upsurge of alcohol consumption and illicit drug use has been accompanied by a proliferation of alcohol- and drug-related problems. Conversely the recent decline in alcohol consumption has been linked with a fall in some alcohol-related problems. The connection between tobacco use and misuse has been vividly demonstrated by the classic study of smoking amongst British doctors that was conducted by Doll and Peto (1976). The availability of a given drug depends upon numerous factors. These include the drug's legal status, price, and methods of production and distribution. Alcohol and tobacco are widely available, and legal subject to rules and regulations which cover their purchase by young people. In North America there has been considerable discussion of the effect of changing the age at which young people can drink in public bars. Several American states have raised this age to 21; this has been noted to have a beneficial effect upon both public drunkenness and the rate of drunken driving amongst young people (e.g. Wagenaar 1981; Williams *et al*. 1982). Ross (1984) has concluded that available evidence related to youthful drunken driving shows 'important safety benefits to be achieved by making the legal drinking age as high as politically feasible' (1984: 114).

Alcohol, being by far the most widely used drug, both in the United Kingdom and elsewhere, is the hardest substance to subject to draconian control policies. Recent opinion polls in Britain indicate a strong popular preference for the legal *status quo*. Opinion favours stricter controls on drunken driving and is positive towards health education. Even so, most people oppose either large price increases or the complete banning of alcohol advertising (Market and Opinion Research International 1980, 1981).

In 1979 the Royal College of Psychiatrists recommended: 'Public review policies of government should be intentionally employed in the interest of health, so as to ensure that per capita alcohol consumption does not increase beyond the present level, and is by stages brought back to an agreed lower level' (1979: 139).

In the same year a confidential British government report on 'Alcohol Policies in the United Kingdom' was produced by the Central Policy Review Staff (or think-tank). This document has not officially been published although an 'unofficial' version has been printed in Sweden. The 'Think-Tank Report' recommended that per capita alcohol consumption in the United Kingdom should not be allowed to increase (Central Policy Review Staff 1979: 90). In fact there is no sign that any political party regards such an approach as attractive material for its manifesto. As the 'Think-Tank Report' noted, alcohol is the concern of many government departments, not the least influential of which appears to be the Treasury. Controlling the level of alcohol consumption poses a political dilemma. This approach to curbing alcohol misuse has been identified as crucial by some of the leading researchers in the field (Bruun *et al.* 1975).

The only official United Kingdom government response to this controversy has been a discussion paper, *Drinking Sensibly*. This rejected proposals to regulate alcohol consumption by controlling price since: 'Government controls capable of influencing the minority who misuse alcohol could not be established without affecting the choices available to the population who drink sensibly' (Department of Health and Social Security 1981: 64–5).

This debate will continue. The health case for preventing alcohol, tobacco, and illicit drugs from becoming cheaper in 'real' terms is a fairly clear one. Other considerations are also relevant and issues such as this are usually resolved on the basis of either public or parliamentary opinion, or both.

Policies to control alcohol, tobacco, or illicit drug use must be realistic and enforceable. Prohibition of alcohol use in America between 1920 and 1933 led to a large fall in alcohol-related problems such as drunkenness convictions and liver cirrhosis deaths. Even so, it provided an unprecedented impetus to organized crime and thereby not only aided bootlegging but laid the foundations for the current distribution network in North America for heroin and other drugs. Ultimately Prohibition foundered because it lacked popular support (Cashman 1981).

Alcohol is widely used and popular. Any policy that resembles Prohibition is pointless and naïvely conceived. Options and evidence relating to alcohol control policies, including controls on drink advertising, have been elaborated elsewhere (Single, Morgan, and de Lint 1981; Makela *et al*. 1981; Grant, Plant, and Williams 1982; Grant and Ritson 1983; Kohn, Smart, and Ogborne 1984).

Responses to alcohol problems, as well as those to tobacco and illicit drug problems, must all come to terms with establishing an acceptable balance between use and misuse. If people: a) like a drug, and b) prefer it to be cheap and accessible, then the price they pay is a higher level of misuse than if the drug is tightly controlled. In essence policies frequently reflect the level of support for drug use. Alcohol has widespread approval in Britain. Tobacco use no longer has such support. This is reflected in the extensions of non-smoking zones in cinemas, theatres, cafés, pubs, trains, and aircraft. In 1984 a total smoking ban was introduced on London underground trains. Such a measure would have been inconceivable ten years before.

Dorn (1980) has reviewed several public opinion polls on cannabis and other illicit drugs. These showed that public sentiment in Britain is overwhelmingly hostile to the use of such substances and strongly supports existing drug laws. It must be noted that controlling the availability of any drug is difficult. If people wish to acquire drugs they often manage to do so. Black markets spring up and illicit drug use is associated with numerous problems such as crime and the dubious quality of the illicit substances. This was evident during Prohibition and applies, on a much smaller scale, to the current use and misuse of illicit drugs in Britain. One surprising development during the period (1979–83) covered by the study described in this book was that the total number of United Kingdom customs staff was *reduced* by over 10 per cent.

It appears that lives are saved whenever the law on drunken driving is visibly and rigorously enforced (Ross 1984; Hingson *et al*. 1984). In addition a recent study of the application of licensing laws in an English town has indicated that comparable benefits may be obtained in relation to several types of crime (Jeffs and Saunders 1983).

The present alcohol, tobacco, and illicit drug laws of the United Kingdom are far from perfect. In spite of this they do broadly reflect public attitudes. There is plenty of scope for applying these laws more rigorously, but this is limited by other often more pressing demands upon those who enforce the law. In addition there is no reason to accept existing laws as immutable or sacrosanct. Legislation can be improved and changed. It is arguable that drunken driving, especially if it inflicts injury or death, warrants far more serious sanctions. Tobacco smoking could probably be banned from many more public places without major public opposition.

Health Education

Education is probably the least controversial line of public policy to curb alcohol, tobacco, and illicit drug misuse. It is not coercive and it is appealing. Many earnest discussions of substance use have concluded that the ideal solution would be to educate young people in particular about the potential dangers of substance misuse. Such education, it is hoped, would enable people to make informed and rational decisions and to avoid dangers. As noted earlier in this chapter, the results of this study do not provide a basis upon which alcohol education may be judged. The study has simply provided confirmation of the already obvious facts that most young adults in Britain drink alcohol and that a large minority also smoke and use illicit drugs. Health education, indeed education in general, should be influenced by these facts. Education is an important arm of public policy towards young people and it is worth considering what this has achieved so far in relation to alcohol, tobacco, and illicit drugs. This appraisal is severely limited since 'education' is not simply something that one receives in a class-room. The majority of school- or college-based educational activities in this field have not been evaluated. In addition some alcohol, drug, and tobacco education has been conducted without explicit objectives.

Alcohol Education

In 1975 an important journal article was published with the title 'The myth of alcoholism prevention'. The author, Kalb, asserted that:

'To talk about prevention belongs in the same category as "Mom and Apple Pie" – everybody is unquestioningly for it, and no one dares to speak out against it. This "sacred cow" philosophy has established a climate in the alcohol field whereby lip service is paid to the importance of prevention programmes but such programmes are not openly and extensively discussed and criticized nor evaluated for their effectiveness.'

(Kalb 1975: 405)

Kalb further lamented that there was almost no worthwhile evidence that alcohol education had been effective.

Five years later Kinder, Pape, and Walfish concluded that alcohol and drug education programmes had been: 'ineffective in obtaining the goals of reducing substance abuse or preventing future abuse. Amongst student populations there is evidence to suggest that these programmes may exacerbate the use and sale of drugs and alcohol' (Kinder, Pape, and Walfish 1980: 1035).

These authors further noted: 'Of the well over 100 published papers to date, a large proportion of these contain no real data upon which to base conclusions regarding the effectiveness of drug/alcohol programmes' (Kinder, Pape, and Walfish 1980: 1036).

A slightly more optimistic tone has been set by Smart, one of the most prolific researchers in the alcohol/drug field:

'Alcohol education, after an undistinguished temperance past, shows signs of being an important part of preventive programmes. Several recent experimental studies have shown beneficial effects over short periods of time. Alcohol education should be expanded to cover more children, and long-term studies of its effectiveness should be planned.

Mass media and mass persuasion alcohol programmes are mostly disappointing in their outcomes. Those that are most effective are associated with some increased enforcement of a new law. Such programmes should be expanded for young people.'

(Smart 1979b: 237).

The results so far produced by alcohol education are largely disappointing. As Smart has noted, some tangible results have been produced, but many studies have failed to demonstrate a significant impact upon either behaviour or attitudes.

A more recent view has been provided by Samuel:

'The prevailing enthusiasm for health and alcohol education has to be a source of bewilderment to those who care to reflect upon it. In the U.K., for example, alcohol education finds its champions in bodies with such diverse and conflicting interests as the Brewers' Society, the Department of Health and Social Security and the Temperance Alliance. If this did not suffice to satisfy the sceptics, alcohol education has been promoted above all other methods of primary prevention despite no evidence to show that it works. . . . Nor is it clear . . . that youthful problem drinking is predictive of problem drinking at a later stage. . . . This raises the possibility that sustained educational attention to something temporary in nature could be both inappropriate and counterproductive.'

(Samuel 1984: 1)

It must be conceded that some studies *have* noted behavioural changes associated with alcohol education. For example, McAlister *et al.* (1980) conducted a follow-up study of alcohol, tobacco, and illicit drug use amongst 526 students at junior high schools in California. They concluded that those who were trained to resist social pressures to drink subsequently reported less frequent alcohol use than those who did not. Even so, such outcomes are greatly outnumbered by negative findings and there appears to be very little 'hard evidence' of such changes. This explains the pessimism of those authors who have reviewed the literature in detail.

Tobacco Education

Tobacco education has a message which in some ways is more clear cut than that of alcohol education. Drinking in moderation is not normally associated with harm (Kreitman 1982). Smoking is unhealthy, and the more one smokes the unhealthier one becomes. The usual message central to tobacco education is simply 'don't smoke'. As noted in Chapter 1, cigarette smoking has become far less popular, and smokers are now in a minority in Britain.

The precise achievements of tobacco education are as hard to assess as are those of alcohol education. This has been conceded by the Royal College of Physicians:

'In both Britain and the U.S.A., although there has been a sub-stantial fall in prevalence and also to a lesser extent in consumption, there is less certainty concerning how this came about. . . . Evaluation of individual anti-smoking campaigns shows that none has ever produced more than a transient effect on smoking pre-valence or consumption. Their value is chiefly in drawing attention to the issue. Each initiative helps to reinforce the image of smoking as an undesirable habit, among both smokers and non-smokers.'

(Royal College of Physicians 1983: 109)

Thompson (1978) reviewed published English-language reports on smoking education programmes that were conducted between 1960 and 1976. She concluded that:

'Most methods used with youth have shown little success. Studies of other methods have shown contradictory results.

    Educational programmes for adults have included large scale anti-smoking campaigns, smoking cessation clinics and a variety of more specific withdrawal methods. . . . Some of these techniques have produced poor results while studies of other methods have shown inconsistent results. The two methods showing most promise are individual counselling and smoking withdrawal clinics.'

(Thompson 1978: 250)

A few studies have been conducted which have indicated that educational programmes may achieve reductions in smoking levels. McAlister *et al.* (1980) concluded that California junior high school students who were trained to cope with pressure to smoke were only half as likely to do so as were those who did not receive such training. Other studies have produced similar results. Aaro *et al.* (1983) reported that anti-smoking campaigns in Norway between 1975 and 1980 led to a decline in smoking when experimental and control groups were compared. These ventures were conducted during a period when youthful smoking was generally decreasing.

Three recent British publications have reported encouraging results from tobacco education campaigns. Dale noted that a campaign amongst schools in Leeds, England, had produced: 'a marked improvement in knowledge, a slight improvement in attitude and equivocal changes in behaviour' (Dale 1978: 142).

Gillies and Wilcox (1984) have described the results from a two-year controlled study of tobacco education. This was conducted amongst 270 9- to 11-year-old children in Sheffield, England. This exercise produced significantly higher levels of knowledge of the dangers of tobacco amongst the experimental group who had participated in the project than amongst the control group who had not. In addition the former reported being significantly less likely to smoke than did the latter. An earlier publication had noted that the same project in Sheffield and Derbyshire, England, had produced beneficial effects upon the smoking behaviour of boys aged 11–12 (Murray *et al.* 1982).

As the Royal College of Physicians (1983) has pointed out, smoking in Britain declined after the publication of each of their two initial reports on the health risks of smoking, but cigarette sales subsequently recovered. It appears very difficult to disentangle the influences which have led to the decline in the proportion of people who smoke. As the Royal College of Physicians has stated, health education comes in many forms:

'"health education" includes all sources of information about the effects of smoking on health. Knowledge originating in scientific journals is gradually passed on to the public through a wide variety of channels, including the media, doctors, nurses, teachers and other professional and non-professional bodies. Through these channels, as well as through overt campaigns mounted by health education specialists, public knowledge of the hazards of smoking to health has steadily grown.'

(Royal College of Physicians 1983: 105)

This is probably perfectly true. It is, nevertheless, speculative. Changes in fashion occur for a multiplicity of reasons. It is possible that the reduction of cigarette smoking has been at least partly encouraged by the increasing variety of alcoholic drinks available, together with the advent of prescribed benzodiazepines and more readily accessible illegal drugs. There is little doubt that recent price increases have hit tobacco sales. In 1984 such increases were explicitly designed by the Chancellor of the Exchequer to discourage smoking.

Drug Education

Conclusions regarding the effectiveness of health education about illicit drugs are at best as doleful as those related to alcohol and tobacco education.

Dorn introduced a review of some drug education issues with the following statement:

'At a recent meeting, experts of the Study Group for the Evaluation of European Drug Education and Policy agreed that, on the basis of the evidence available from evaluations throughout the world, no known methods of drug education can be said to reduce drug use. Claims of successful reduction in drug use have generally come from unevaluated programmes or from evaluations of poor design – the more rigorous the evaluation, the less likely it was to provide evidence of reduction in drug use.'

(Dorn 1981b: 281–82)

Schaps et al. (1981) reviewed 127 drug education programmes. They concluded that only minor results had been achieved by any of these.

Bandy and President have concurred with this view:

'Despite the fact that there have been many health-related mass media campaigns conducted during recent years, researchers note that it is difficult to assess their impact. . . . Few campaigns have been evaluated well; many are described in inaccessible internal reports and others have not been documented at all. Of those evaluated campaigns aimed at changing attitudes and behaviours, only a few have demonstrated successful change.

(Bandy and President 1983: 266)

This comment was an echo of that made nine years earlier by Goodstadt (1974). Even so, Goodstadt added an important word of caution and advice:

'the current evidence makes it equally unwarranted to conclude that drug education has had no impact or that it has had a negative effect by encouraging drug use. Future research is needed which meets a higher scientific standard (the difficulty of which is not under-estimated), enabling those involved in drug education to acquire more confident insights into the effects of their activities.'

(Goodstadt 1974: 144)

One of the most recent contributions to the drug education debate has been provided by the Advisory Council on the Misuse of Drugs (1984). In a report entitled *Prevention* it was noted: 'Because there are many pathways leading toward drug misuse, some of which have not yet been identified or fully understood, there are a variety of potential preventative measures' (1984: 13).

The Advisory Council stated that health education techniques used to foster the abandonment of smoking may be inappropriate in relation to illicit drugs. The Advisory Council also emphasized the following in relation to the Health Education Council (for England and Wales):

'We understand that the Council feels that caution should be exercised in the use of widespread publicity on drug misuse, partly because of uncertainty over the size of the problem in Britain, and partly because of the risk that ill-chosen educational methods attach disproportionate importance to drug misuse and arouse in some people an interest which they would not otherwise have felt.'

(Advisory Council on the Misuse of Drugs 1984: 17)

Sadly this advice failed to deter the British government from mounting a 'high profile' mass-media anti-drug campaign during 1985. This was undertaken in defiance of a considerable body of informed opinion.

The Role of Education

The preceding assessments of alcohol, tobacco, and illicit drug education make depressing reading. Educational initiatives aimed at 'normal' people have had little demonstrable impact in changing either their behaviour or their attitudes. Education is not a panacea and this is hardly surprising. The wide variety of factors that influence the use and misuse of legal and illegal drugs has been briefly indicated earlier in this chapter. Education cannot be expected to compensate for peer pressure, personal problems, hedonism, biological, or psychological predispositions, or the widespread availability of cheap psychoactive drugs. Neither can educationalists be expected to carry the sins of the world on their shoulders nor to compensate for public or political reluctance to modify laws or to control the availability of drugs which are misused.

Although many educational initiatives have now been conducted, reviews of these bleakly conclude that the great majority have neither been well constructed nor properly evaluated. There is little to suggest that this situation is improving. The Health Education Council recently conducted an expensive media campaign on alcohol use and misuse in the north-east of England. This venture, as noted by Grant (1982a), had many excellent features and was a refreshing change from some of the negative approaches adopted in similar campaigns. An assessment of this exercise reported that it was not possible to evaluate the effects of the campaign thoroughly because no adequate research strategy had been employed to facilitate this (Health Education Council 1983).

Education is important. It is important as a symbolic statement that society is concerned about alcohol, tobacco, and illicit drug problems. It is important that available knowledge should be disseminated as widely as possible. Young people, the population at large, those in the 'helping professions', journalists, and politicians are all legitimate and important target groups for health education. It is possible to inform people about the range of services available to help problem drinkers and those with other drug problems (Plant, Pirie, and Kreitman 1979). Educational/behavioural approaches appear most fruitful as a means of helping those with alcohol and other drug problems to overcome or to control their difficulties (e.g. Heather and Robertson 1981; Grant 1984c).

It would be totally unjustified on the basis of current evidence to discard education as a response to youthful (or other) substance misuse. Clearly education in this field does not seem to have achieved very much. Future initiatives need to be conducted with care and on an experimental basis. Aims and methods need to be selected, following the guidance of available world-wide evidence. Evaluation must be taken seriously and should be conducted with openness and rigour. Agencies spending large sums of public money must demonstrate that they are attempting to spend it in a constructive way. Mass-media campaigns are often mounted to demonstrate that action is being taken. In fact there is little to commend them. Other, far cheaper, approaches are usually preferable. This raises an important point. Many initiatives are undertaken which are really propaganda and not education. Educationalists frequently have pressure exerted on them by their political masters who find media campaigns attractive simply because of their visibility. Some newspaper, radio, and television coverage continues to be ill-informed, grossly alarmist, and oversensationalized. For example some news reporting has virtually advertised the once rare practice of glue and solvent sniffing. The spread of this activity may well have been assisted by detailed and lurid accounts which have described not only potentially 'sniffable' agents, but also how to (mis)use them.

One role of health educationalists should be to inform others of what has and what may be achieved by education in this field. This message does not yet seem to have been imparted to many people. It is still widely and wrongly believed that such education is routinely effective in leading people to drink less and to abstain from other drugs. Unrealistic expectations of health education may serve to distract attention from other, possibly far more fruitful, policy options.

THE PRACTICAL APPLICATIONS OF THIS STUDY

Throughout this book attention has been drawn to the quality of the information obtained. This is examined further in Appendix 3. Although, for many purposes, the information is acceptable, it can only be regarded as a crude approximation to a limited range of measures of real-life events. Drinking, smoking, and illicit drug use are all complex forms of behaviour and the information collected in this study serves to re-emphasize, rather than to explain, this complexity.

'Epidemiology' is literally the study of the mass aspects of disease. In relation to the use and misuse of alcohol, tobacco, and illicit drugs, surveys are a useful, if limited, means of generating epidemiological information. Surveys such as that described in this book serve a useful role in providing an account of alcohol, tobacco, and illicit drug use amongst a 'normal' group of people. Such exercises are useful since to understand psychoactive drug problems would be extremely difficult if one were confined to information about drug-dependent individuals in contact with 'official agencies' such as alcohol problem clinics or drug dependence clinics. Responses to the inappropriate, excessive, or harmful use of psychoactive drugs require the guidance of the fullest amount of information possible.

What is the relevance of this follow-up survey? It was an exercise concerned with describing the changing drinking, smoking, and illicit drug-taking habits of a group of Scottish school-leavers. The results obtained only form a basis for generalization to the extent that they agree or differ with evidence from other sources. Patterns of psycho-active drug use vary between different localities, age groups, and times. Since the third phase of this study was completed in 1983 it appears that illicit drug use in Britain has continued to rise considerably, while the consumption of both alcohol and tobacco has continued to decline. This survey is already out of date since it does not describe alcohol, tobacco, and illicit drug use at the time you read this book. Nor can it be assumed that the same results would have been obtained had the study group been located not in the Lothian Region, but in the United States, Wales, or Finland. These qualifications are important when assessing the implications of this exercise.

Possibly the most forbidding result of this study was the high level of illicit drug use that was evident amongst the young unemployed. This is consistent with growing evidence of the harmful effects of unemploy-ment (Platt and Kreitman 1984). Economic forecasts are not optimistic about the levels of unemployment to be expected during the next few years and it would appear that illicit drugs are becoming cheaper to obtain. It is therefore reasonable to expect that illicit drug use will continue to rise in future as it has been doing steadily in the past twenty years. In fact at the time of writing evidence suggests that illicit drug use is spreading at an accelerated rate. This study confirms existing evidence that many young alcohol misusers are also polydrug users. Urgency is therefore lent to the need for more facilities to help such people. Increasingly, existing agencies for the treatment of alcohol-related problems being confronted with a demand to help people whose difficulties relate not solely to alcohol, but to several types of drug. Only in large cities can specialized services for alcohol, drug, or even tobacco problems be provided. In smaller communities service provision should increasingly be geared to help the problem drug taker, regardless of the type of drug or drugs he or she uses. Some agencies, such as local councils on alcoholism, have already responded to this need. Others should be encouraged to follow suit. In essence this means that the existing agencies established to help problem drinkers should increasingly open their doors, if they do not do so already, to help people with problems related not only to alcohol but to other substances. In many instances such an adaptation will require additional funding because of greater demands upon agencies. Even so, the alcohol services which are already well developed form the logical basis of the infrastructure upon which to build a more general range of drug services. In addition the essential skills required to help problem drinkers are very similar to those needed to counsel and assist those with problems related to other drugs.

It is acknowledged that some agencies, or rather the people who operate them, will not wish to change in this way. Experience in combining alcohol and drug services is variable. Some people in the alcohol problems field may be less eager to work with illicit drug problems. It is unrealistic to expect either uniformity in service provision or that all of those in the statutory and non-statutory services will wish to conform to any central dictat.

A final plea is advanced. Alcohol, tobacco, and drug-related problems are almost certainly here to stay. Patterns of use will ebb and flow, and cannot usefully be predicted. Even so future responses should be influenced by available evidence and by past experience. No country can afford to be insular in devising responses. These must be designed upon the basis of what international evidence has to offer. In addition they must be conducted experimentally and should, as far as possible, be properly and independently evaluated. In a world of scarce resources and conflicting priorities there is no need to repeat old mistakes or to waste time and money. Evaluation needs to be taken seriously and accorded a high priority. At present it is not. Most people use alcohol, or illicit drugs, in moderation. The price to be paid for such widespread moderate use is a greater level of harm for a minority of people. This situation demands a rational, balanced response.

Appendix 1: The Self-completed Questionnaire (Waves One and Two)

During the first two waves of this study, data were collected from a self-completed schedule. The questions included in this instrument are summarized below.*

1   Please indicate whether you are male or female.

2   In which country were you born?

3   With whom do you live?

4   How many brothers and sisters do you have?

5   (*Only answer if you do have any brothers or sisters.*)
     Are any of them older than you?

6(a) What sort of work does your father/stepfather usually do?
      (*Write in.*)
  (b) Is this a manual or a non-manual job?
  (c) Is your father/stepfather working or unemployed at present?

7(a) Does your mother/stepmother have a job?
  (b) (*Answer only if she has a job.*)
      Is this a manual or a non-manual job?

8(a) Have you always lived with both of your parents?
  (b) (*Only answer if you have not.*) Why is this?
  (c) (*Only answer if you have not always lived with both parents.*)
      Until what age did you live with both parents?

9   What is your religion?

*The full instruments used in this study are available from the authors.

10   Does your father/stepfather ever drink alcohol, even occasionally?

11   Does your mother/stepmother ever drink alcohol, even occasionally?

12   Would your father/stepfather mind if you drank alcohol?

13   Would your mother/stepmother mind if you drank alcohol?

14   Has your father/stepfather ever told you that he does not want you to start drinking?

15   Has your mother/stepmother ever told you that she does not want you to start drinking?

16   Has your father/stepfather ever offered you a drink?

17   Has your mother/stepmother ever offered you a drink?

18   Have you ever been in disagreement with your parents/step-parents because of drink?

19(a)   Have you received any information, or had any lessons or discussions about alcohol and drinking while you were in school?
   (b)   Have you ever been shown a film about alcohol or drinking in school?
   (c)   If alcohol or drinking have been mentioned in school, please tick those subjects in which this has occurred.

English	Religion/scripture
Mathematics	Woodwork/metalwork
History	Technical drawing
Geography	Civics
Biology/anatomy/	Typing
physiology/health etc.	Sewing
Science	French/German/Latin etc.
Art	Music
Physical education/sports	Other subjects — write in what
Domestic science/cookery	

20   Have you ever received any information about alcohol or drinking from any of the following people? (Tick either 'yes' or 'no' for each.)

(a) A doctor or nurse
(b) A teacher
(c) A person from the church
(d) A special health visitor
(e) Your parents
(f) On television*
(g) Anybody else (write in)

21   Have you ever tasted an alcoholic drink (including cider, shandy, beer, lager, whisky, port, sherry, Guinness, Mackeson, Martini, wine, rum, gin, vodka, or other spirits)?

(For people who have ever tasted an alcoholic drink)

22   How old were you when you had your *first* taste of alcohol?

23   Who gave you your first taste of alcohol?

24   Below is a list of places where people sometimes have a drink. Tick each of these where you have had a drink.

(a) In your own home
(b) In the home of adult relatives or friends of your parents
(c) In a public house or hotel
(d) In the home of one of your own friends
(e) At a dance
(f) In the open air somewhere, such as a street or park
(g) Elsewhere – write in

25   Which of the following drinks have you tried? Tick all those that you have ever tried.

Beer ('heavy', 'light ale')	Gin
Lager	Rum
Stout (including Guinness, Mackeson)	Brandy
	Martini
Cider	Sherry
Shandy	Port
Whisky	Other wines
Vodka	Anything else? Write in what

*This item was only used in the second wave of data collection.

26   Which is your usual or favourite type of drink?

27   When did you last have a drink?

28   Who were you with when you last had a drink?

29   Where were you when you last had a drink?

30   *Think about the last time you had a drink.*
       Exactly how much did you drink on that occasion?
   (a) How many *pints* of beer, lager, cider, shandy, stout, etc. did you drink?
   (b) How many *single glasses* of whisky, vodka, gin, rum, or other spirits did you drink?
   (c) How many *single glasses* of Martini, port, sherry, or wine did you drink?

31   The last time you had a drink, did you drink more, less, or about the same as usual?

32   Think carefully back over the last seven days.
       Please write in exactly what alcoholic drinks you have consumed on each day during the past week. For each day write in:
    i) The number of *pints* of beer, lager, cider, shandy, stout, etc.
   ii) The number of *single glasses* of whisky, vodka, gin, rum, etc.
  iii) The number of *single glasses* of Martini, port, sherry, or wine etc. that you have drunk. Try to remember where you were and who you were with on each day. This may help you remember what you have had to drink.

33(a) Would you say that last week was fairly typical of what you usually have to drink in a week?
   (b) If last week was not typical, would you normally drink more or less in a week?

34   Below is given a list of ways people sometimes feel after they have been drinking. Read through the list and put a tick to show *how often you have felt like that* when you have been drinking.

       (a) Happy
       (b) Sad
       (c) 'Bigger', more self-confident
       (d) Sick

(e) Feel like smashing things
(f) Feel warm
(g) Feel like a fight or an argument

35   Below is a list of reasons *why people drink*. Put a tick by each item to show whether that reason is TRUE or FALSE *for you*.

(a) I like the taste
(b) So as not to be the 'odd one out' in a group
(c) To calm my nerves and help me relax
(d) To give myself courage and confidence
(e) It helps me to talk to members of the opposite sex more easily
(f) So that my friends won't think I'm scared or 'yellow'
(g) To help me mix more easily with other people
(h) To help me stop worrying about something

36(a) Have you ever been 'merry', 'a little bit drunk' or 'very drunk'?
 (b) If you have, fill in the following table to show how many times you have been 'merry', 'a little bit drunk' or 'very drunk' *in the last six months*.

   i) Just 'merry' or 'happy'
   ii) 'A little bit drunk'
   iii) 'Very drunk'

37(a) Have you ever had a hangover?
 (b) *If you have*, how many times have you had a hangover *in the last six months*?

38   Please tick 'yes' or 'no' to *each* of the following questions:

(a) Have people annoyed you by criticizing your drinking?
(b) Have you ever had problems at school because of your drinking?
(c) Has your doctor ever advised you not to drink as much as you do?
(d) Have you ever spent more money than you ought to on drink?
(e) Have you ever had trouble or quarrels with family or friends because of your drinking?
(f) Have you ever had money problems because of your drinking?
(g) Have you ever had an accident or hurt yourself because of your drinking?

(h) Have you ever had a drink first thing in the morning to steady your nerves or to get rid of a hangover?

(i) After drinking have you found your hand shaky in the morning?

(j) Have you ever arrived late for school due to a hangover?

(k) Have you ever missed a day's school due to a hangover?

(l) Have you ever had an upset stomach because of drinking?

(m) Has your drinking ever worried you?

(n) Has your drinking ever caused you problems?

(Only answer Questions 39–42 if you have never tasted an alcoholic drink)

39   If someone offers you a drink, do you often feel embarrassed when you refuse it?

40   Read through the questions below and then put a tick by each one to show *how often* these happen to you.

(a) If someone offers you a drink how often are you tempted to try it?

(b) When you are at a party where people are drinking do you ever feel 'left out' of things?

(c) When you go out with friends of your own age, about how often are you offered a drink?

(d) Do your friends ever urge you to try 'just a little one' or try to persuade you to have a drink?

41   Below is a list of reasons why people do *not* drink. Read through the list and tick each item to show whether that reason is TRUE or FALSE *for you*.

(a) I don't like the taste

(b) Drinking is unhealthy and makes you ill

(c) Drinking costs too much

(d) People who drink are wicked

(e) Drinking is against my religion

(f) Drinking makes people lose control of themselves

(g) Drinking is evil

(h) Once you start drinking you can't stop the habit

(i)   My parents disapprove strongly of anyone who drinks

(j)   Some other reason (write what)

42   Do you think you may start drinking when you get older?

(The remaining questions are to be answered by everyone.)

43   Have you every had a stomach ulcer?

44   Have you ever had liver trouble?

45   Have you ever tried any of the following either from curiosity or for kicks?

(a)   Cannabis ('pot', marijuana, 'dope', 'grass', 'hash')

(b)   LSD ('acid', lysergic acid diethylamide$_{25}$)

(c)   Barbiturates

(d)   Mogadon

(e)   Librium

(f)   Valium

(g)   Glues, solvents, dry-cleaning fluids (by sniffing)

(h)   Amphetamines (pep pills)

(i)   Opium

(j)   Morphine

(k)   Heroin

(l)   Cocaine

(m)   Sleeping-tablets/tranquillizers

(n)   Other drugs (write what)

46(a)   Have you ever tried smoking tobacco (either in cigarettes, cigars, or a pipe)?

(b)   About how many cigarettes do you smoke now?

(c)   If a friend offered you a cigarette would you smoke it?

47   People have many different ideas about alcohol and drinking. Below is a list of ideas. We want to know whether you agree or disagree with them.

Sometimes you may *agree strongly*. Sometimes you may *disagree strongly*. At times you may just *agree* or *disagree*. You may be *uncertain*. Read each item and put a tick to show how strongly you agree or disagree with each one. There are no 'right' or 'wrong' answers.

(a)   If you don't go in pubs you are missing a lot of fun

(b)   Boys and girls who drink know how to look after themselves

(c) Drinking makes you feel on top of the world

(d) Drinking can help people when they feel nervous or embarrassed

(e) Girls who drink get more dates than girls who do not drink

(f) It worries me that so many grown-ups cannot stop drinking

(g) Drinking alcohol is not dangerous for teenagers

(h) Even if you *do* drink, it's best to try to stay out of pubs

(i) The age limit for drinking in public houses should be lowered from 18 to 16 years

(j) Drinking makes you feel more at ease

(k) Young people who drink are more attractive than those who don't

(l) People who drink cause trouble and get into fights fairly often

(m) It's only natural and right for a man to like his beer

(n) Adults only try to stop you drinking because they don't like to see you enjoying yourself

(o) There is nothing wrong with drinking

(p) It's the boys who drink who get all the girls

(q) People who drink are usually more friendly than people who don't

(r) Students who get caught drinking at school should be punished severely

(s) It's mainly the reckless boys and girls who start drinking regularly while they are still at school

(t) There's something mature and manly about boys who drink

You have already told us something about yourself. Now we would like you to tell us *what you think of other teenagers*. Think first about **teenagers who drink heavily.**

Here is a practice question about teenagers *who drink heavily.*

Talk a lot [   ] [   ]   ?   [   ] [   ] Do not talk much   ?

If you think teenagers who drink heavily *talk a lot*, put a tick in the box at the *far left*.

If you think teenagers who drink heavily *do not talk much*, put a tick in the box at the *far right*.

Most people know which of these two kinds of thing to choose, but if you cannot decide, put a tick in one of the centre boxes. Use the left centre box if you think teenagers who drink heavily *tend to talk a lot*. If you think teenagers who drink heavily *tend not to talk much*, use the *right centre box*. If you really cannot decide which to choose, put a circle round the question mark.

The question above was just a practice question. Now tick each of the following questions using the box which is right for **the teenager who drinks heavily**.

[THE FORMAT GIVEN ABOVE WAS USED IN THE FOLLOWING QUESTIONS]

48   **The teenager who drinks heavily**

(a)	Happy	Sad
(b)	Rough	Gentle
(c)	Has a lot of friends	Has a few friends
(d)	Usually successful	Usually unsuccessful
(e)	Interested in the opposite sex	Not interested in the opposite sex
(f)	Relaxed	Tense
(g)	Hard	Not so hard
(h)	Good at schoolwork	Not so good at schoolwork
(i)	Likes to do forbidden things	Does not like to do forbidden things
(j)	Attractive	Not so attractive
(k)	Easy going	Takes life rather seriously
(l)	Smart and tidy	Not very smart and tidy
(m)	Sharp	Dull
(n)	Acts on the spur of the moment	Stops to think before acting
(o)	Able to attract members of the opposite sex	Does not attract members of the opposite sex

In the last part, you told us about the kind of teenager who drinks heavily. Will you now think about **the kind of teenager who does not drink?**

The questions are the same, but this time we want to know about the teenager *who does NOT drink*.

Think about each item carefully, and then tick each of the following questions, using the box which is right for the kind of teenager *who does NOT drink*.

49   **The teenager who does not drink**
[The categories in Q.49 are identical with those in Q.48.]

50   About how many of your friends drink alcohol?

51   We are interested in which school subjects you like or dislike. Below is a list of subjects. Please tick each of these subjects *that you yourself take* to show whether you like or dislike it or whether you *neither* like nor dislike it. If you *do not* do any of these subjects do not tick them.

English	Religion/scripture
Mathematics	Woodwork/metalwork
History	Technical drawing
Geography	Civics
Biology/anatomy/	Typing
physiology/health etc.	Sewing
Science	French/German/Latin etc.
Art	Music
Physical education/sports	Other subjects
Domestic science/cookery	

52   (a) When you leave school do you want to begin work straight away, or do you want to go to college or university?

      (b) What type of work do you eventually want to do?

      (c) Is that a manual or a non-manual job?

53   (a) Do you have any hobbies or spare-time interests?

      (b) *If you do*, what are these? (Write in)

      (c) Is it usual for you to have a drink in connection with any of these hobbies or spare-time interests?

      (d) Is drinking a regular part of your free time?

Please PRINT your *full* name clearly below.
Please PRINT your *full* home address.
What is your date of birth?
Please write in the names and addresses of *two* relatives or close friends through whom we could contact you in future if you move from your present address.
Thank you very much for your help with this study.

Appendix 2: The Interview Schedule (Wave Three)

During the third wave of this study data were collected by trained interviewers administering a standardized interview schedule. The questions included in this instrument are summarized below.

1 How long ago did you leave school?

2 Can you tell me exactly what you have done since you left school – starting from the month you left?

3 **SHOWCARD A**   GIVE SHOWCARD TO RESPONDENT
   So what you are doing right now can best be described as:

   YOP (Youth Opportunities Programme) or other government scheme
   Full-time work (30+ hours per week)
   Part-time work (8–29 hours per week)
   Unemployed and seeking work
   Unemployed and not seeking work
   Mother/housewife (not more than 7 hours' work outside home per week) and not seeking work
   Full-time education
   Part-time education
   Part-time education and part-time work
   Temporarily laid off
   Disability and no job to go back to
   Temporarily out of work due to illness/disability and job to go back to
   Other (please specify)

4   And have you been doing this for

over 24 months?	4–6 months
13–23 months	1–3 months
7–12 months	less than 1 month?

5   ASK **all** RESPONDENTS WHO HAVE **at any time** BEEN
EMPLOYED

What is your occupation, that is, your present main paid job or
(if does not have one now) your last main paid job?

Is it an apprenticeship?

6   Why did you leave your last job?

7   ALL RESPONDENTS
Have you taken any exams?
If yes, ask
Do you have any of the following:

Taken exams but not passed any
CSEs
'O' levels
Highers or 'A' levels
City and Guilds
ONC, HND
Other (please specify)

8   What is the main source of your income at the moment?

9   How much money did you have to live on last week (after
stoppages of tax, National Insurance)?

10   How much money did you have left to spend after your rent, food,
and keep were paid for last week?

11   MARITAL STATUS

Are you?	Separated
Single	Widowed
Cohabiting	Divorced
Married	

12   QUESTION REFERS TO PERSONS RESIDING AT RESPONDENT'S
PLACE OF ABODE AND NOT TO MARITAL STATUS
Who do you live (stay) with?

13   Who brought you up?

14   IF MALE HEAD OF HOUSEHOLD INVOLVED IN UPBRINGING OF
RESPONDENT, REFER TO HIM, AS APPROPRIATE, AND ASK:
    Is the male head of household in which you grew up still alive?
    If no, When did he die?

15   What is (or was) your father's/stepfather's/guardian's present or
last main paid job?

16   Was he ever unemployed in the last two years?
    If yes, ask How many times?
     (i) How much time is that altogether?
    (ii) Is he employed now?

17   IF FEMALE HEAD OF HOUSEHOLD INVOLVED IN UPBRINGING
OF RESPONDENT, ASK:
    Is the female head of household in which you grew up still alive?
    If no, When did she die?

18   What is (or was) your mother's/stepmother's/guardian's present
or last main paid job?

19   Was she ever unemployed in the past two years?
    If yes, ask How many times?
        (i) How much time is that altogether?
       (ii) Is she unemployed now?

20   Do you have any brothers or sisters?
    If yes, How many?

21   Do you have any children?
    If yes, How many?

22   In what kind of housing do you live?

        Privately owned house/flat
        Privately rented house/flat
        Council house/flat
        College/University housing
        Digs/lodgings
        Housing Association
        HM Armed Forces
        Tied to occupation, e.g. policeman

Hospital/hostel/residential centre
Other (please specify)

23   Suppose you had a personal problem. Is there anyone you could talk it over with?
    If yes
    Can you talk quite freely with him/her? Can you tell everything, even the most personal things?
    Can you always get hold of him or her? Is he/she always around to talk to if you have a problem?
    Do you think he/she tells you his/her worries?

24   Have you drunk any alcohol at all in the last two years?
    If no, ask Have you ever drunk alcohol?
    If has drunk but not in past two years, ask
    Why did you stop drinking alcohol? Were you having drinking problems?

25   How often do you usually have a drink containing alcohol?

26   When did you last have a drink containing alcohol?

27   Think about the last time you had even one drink of alcohol. Exactly what did you drink and how much of it?

TIME = SEPARATE DRINKING SESSION – A GAP OF TWO HOURS TERMINATES A SESSION

Who were you with on this occasion – that is, when you last had a drink?

Nobody, drinking alone
Parents/stepparents/guardians
Siblings
Other relatives
Spouse/cohabitee/boyfriend/girlfriend
Friend(s) – same sex
Friend(s) – opposite sex
Friends – both sexes
Workmates
Other (specify)

And where were you?

28   **If drunk alcohol in past seven days, ask**
Now I need to find out about your drinking over the past seven days, what exactly you were drinking, how much, and when. Starting with yesterday, between what times were you drinking, what did you drink and how much?
What is a typical week?

29   How many days in the past two years have you had more than 3 pints of beer, **or** more than 6 measures of spirits, **or** more than 6 glasses of wine, **or** their equivalent, during one drinking session?
IF *never* IN PREVIOUS QUESTION, PROCEED TO Q.30
Otherwise ask
(i) How many days in the past 2 years have you had 10 pints of beer **or** 20 measures of spirits **or** 20 glasses (2 bottles) of wine, **or** their equivalent during one drinking session?
(ii) Think back to the last time you had that amount, that is 10 pints of beer or its equivalent. [IF *never* IN Q.29 (i) **ask** SAME ABOUT 3 PINTS OF BEER OR ITS EQUIVALENT.] What was happening? What kind of an occasion was it?

30   In the past year, has there been any increase or decrease in the amount of time you spend on drinking?
When do you tend to drink more? When you are with friends of same sex or when you are in mixed company?

31   ALL RESPONDENTS, INCLUDING THOSE WHO HAVE NOT DRUNK IN PAST TWO YEARS, RETURN AT THIS POINT.
Ask drinkers
Do you drink less, the same, or more now than your friends of the same sex?
Ask non-drinkers (WHO HAVE NOT DRUNK IN PAST TWO YEARS)
Are your friends of the same sex mainly drinkers or non-drinkers like you?

32   Now to some questions about your health. Have you had stomach or duodenal ulcers in the past two years?
If yes
Does alcohol make it worse?
If no
Has anyone else suggested that it does?

33   Have you had gastritis (inflamed stomach) in the past two years?
If yes
Does alcohol make it worse?
If no
Has anyone else, e.g. a doctor, suggested that alcohol makes it worse? What do you think?

34   In the past two years, have you ever noticed that you sweat excessively in the later part of the night or upon waking in the morning when you have been drinking the day before (or when there has been a change in your drinking)?
If yes
How often has this happened in past three months?

35   It is quite a common experience amongst people who once in a while have a good drink to notice their hands tremble the next morning. Has this ever happened to you?
If yes
Have you noticed this happening in the past three months?
If yes
How often?
Does this trembling ever make it difficult to hold a glass? Did it happen more than once? Have your legs or whole body shaken?

36   Have you ever had a really terrible hangover?
If yes
When was the last time this happened?
Did it bother you? Or did it make any problems?

37   In the past two years, have you ever had a drink soon after waking in order to help you relax and settle yourself, or to cure a hangover?
If yes
How often in past three months?
Ask all respondents
What is the shortest time after waking up that you have had a drink?

38   In the past two years, have there been certain situations or times of the day when you felt restless or irritable without a drink?

If yes
How often has this been happening in the past three months?

Would others notice you feeling restless?
Does this restlessness interfere with what you are doing?

39   In the past two years, have you tried to cut down your drinking?
If yes
How difficult did you find it?
If very difficult
Was it impossible?
If difficult
Was this because of the way you felt, or because of pressure by others?

40   **Ask only respondents who have tried to cut down drinking in past two years**
What was your main reason for trying to cut down your drinking?

41   **All respondents**
In the past two years, have there been any occasions or situations where you especially intended to avoid drinking much or drinking at all?
If yes
Were you able to stop yourself drinking?
If difficult
How many times in the past three months have you found it difficult to stop yourself drinking when you had meant not to drink? Was this because of the way you felt or because of pressure by others?

42   In the past two years, have you been injured in any kind of accident?
If yes
How many times?
For any of these accidents, had *you* been drinking?
If yes
Do you think your drinking was responsible?
If no
Did anyone else suggest it?

IF RESPONDENT ASCRIBES ACCIDENT TO OWN DRINKING, PROCEED TO Q.43 BELOW, **otherwise ask**
Were you with someone who had been drinking?
If yes

Do you think that person's drinking was responsible for the accident?

43 **All respondents**
In the past two years, have you given up or have you spent less time on any activities, hobbies or spare-time interests because of drinking?
If yes
Why did this happen? Was it mainly a question of time, money, or something else perhaps?

44 Do you often feel depressed or low?
IF NO, PROCEED TO Q.45 BELOW.
Otherwise ask
Is it ever after drinking alcohol?
If yes
How often has this happened in the past three months?

45 Have you ever drunk alcohol to cheer yourself up?
If yes
How often have you done this in the past three months?

46 **To female respondents only, ask**
Have you ever drunk alcohol during your period to buck yourself up?
If yes
How often have you done this in the past two years?

47 **Ask all respondents**
Have you ever taken an overdose of tablets or made any form of suicide attempt?
If yes
Was it in the past two years?
If yes
Did alcohol have anything to do with it?
If no
Did someone else perhaps think it did?

48 Where you live (or have lived) have there ever been arguments or complaints about your drinking?
If yes
When was the last occasion?

How do these arguments (or nagging) affect you?
Does it bother you?

49   In the rows you have (or have had) with your family or *whoever you have lived with*, has anyone ever hit anybody else for any reason?
If yes
When was the last occasion?
Who did the hitting?
If self
Do you think that your drinking was in some way responsible?
If no
Did any other person think that your drinking was in some way responsible?

50   Have any arguments with whomever you live with ever led to:

  (i) *Your* being asked to leave?
 (ii) Such an unpleasant atmosphere that you thought of leaving?
(iii) Others threatening to leave you?

IF 'NO' TO **all** ABOVE, PROCEED TO QUESTION 51 **otherwise ask**
When was the last occasion something like that happened?
Did you/he/she/they actually leave?
Was drinking in any way responsible for the split-up or the threats to split up?
If no
Would someone else claim alcohol responsible?
Does splitting up, or the thought of it, bother or upset you?

51   Have you ever got into trouble and been asked to leave any of the following places?

Buses/trains
Disco/dance halls
Licensed club, bar, pub, hotel
Homes of friends, friends' parents, family
Soccer or rugby matches
Clubs
Shops
Cinema/pictures
Other (please specify)

IF NO TO **all**, PROCEED TO Q. 52 BELOW
If yes to any, ask
How often has this happened in the past two years?

IF HAPPENED IN LAST TWO YEARS, **ask all** OF FOLLOWING
QUESTIONS
(i) On the occasions when this has happened, how often was **your** drinking responsible?
(ii) Think back to the very last occasion: was **your** drinking in some way involved?
If no, ask
Did someone else, e.g. the person who asked you to leave, believe that *your* drinking was responsible?
(iii) At that last occasion, did you get into trouble or were you asked to leave because you were under age?
(iv) Did the whole experience bother you much?

52   In the past two years have you been absent from work for a day or more through feeling unwell?
IF NO, PROCEED TO Q.53
Otherwise ask
Were you ever absent for any reason connected with drinking, like a bad hangover?
If no, ask
Did someone else ever claim you were absent because of a hangover?
IF ASCRIBED BY SELF OR OTHER, ASK
(i) When was the last time this happened?
(ii) Did it bother you or cause you any problems at work or home?

53   In the past two years, have you ever been late for work (class)?
IF NO, PROCEED TO Q.54
Otherwise ask
Was it for any reason connected with drinking, like a hangover?
If no, ask
Perhaps you don't agree, but did someone else say your lateness was due to your drinking?
If no, ask
Did someone else ever claim you were absent because of a hangover?

If ascribed by self or other, ask
 (i) When was the last time this happened?
 (ii) Did it bother you or cause any problems at work or home?

54   Have you ever left or had to leave a job?
IF NO, PROCEED TO Q.55
If yes, ask
On the only/last occasion on which it happened, was drink in any way involved?
If no, ask
You may not agree, but did anyone else, e.g. your boss or family, say that drink was in some way responsible?

55   Some people get into quite heated rows while they are drinking. Does this ever happen to you?
IF NEVER, PROCEED TO Q.56
If yes, ask
When was the last occasion this happened?
Do you think drink is responsible for these rows?
If no, ask
Does someone else say drinking is responsible? Do you worry about them? Are they a problem in your life?

56   Have you ever got into physical fights while drinking?
IF NEVER, PROCEED TO Q.57
If yes, ask
When was the last occasion?
Is it a matter of concern for you? Do you worry about it?

57   When you have been drinking, have you ever injured yourself or others in a fight?
IF NEVER, PROCEED TO Q.58
If yes, ask
When was the last occasion?
Did it bother you?

58   **If respondent has brother(s) or sister(s), ask**
Were your brother(s) or sister(s) ever affected by your drinking?

59   **If respondent has own child(ren), ask**
Was your own child(ren) ever affected by your drinking?

60 **Ask all respondents**
Have you ever got into financial difficulties because of drinking?
(Do not include being short of money during or immediately after
a drinking session.)
If yes, ask
How did you manage?

61 **SHOWCARD B**   GIVE SHOWCARD TO RESPONDENT
People often do things when they drink which they regret later.
Here's a card listing some of these things. Have any of them
happened to you in the past two years? You can just answer 'yes' or
'no' for each letter in turn.

(a) Said something to someone you later regretted
(b) Been sexually involved with someone, and regretted later
(c) Been very loud and noisy, and later regretted it
(d) Been destructive or aggressive, and later regretted it
(e) Become weepy, and later regretted it
(f) Got pregnant, or got someone pregnant, and regretted it
(g) Been sick or passed out when others were around, and
     regretted it later
(h) Unable to perform as well as expected to because of drinking,
     e.g. at exams, sports, sex
(i) Unable to remember what you did or said, and embarrassed
     when told later
(j) Broke the law or committed some minor misdemeanour, and
     regretted it later
(k) Anything else (please specify)

If yes to any item on showcard, ask
When was the last time any of the above happened?

62 **Ask all respondents**
In the past two years, have you ever been helped by or sought help
from any of the following?

GP/Other doctor apart from psychiatrist
Psychiatrist/Psychologist
Council on Alcoholism, AA, Drinkwatchers
Family or friends
Teacher/Minister of religion
Social worker
Other (please specify)

63   Have you ever been helped or sought help for drinking?
IF NO, PROCEED TO Q.64 BELOW
If yes, ask
Did you go to or were you helped by any of the following?

GP/Other doctor apart from psychiatrist
Psychiatrist/Psychologist
Council on Alcoholism, Drinkwatchers,
      AA, or any other group
Teacher/Minister of Religion
Family/friends
Social Worker
Other (please specify)

Why did you seek or get help? Can you name the single most important reason?

64   Have you ever been referred to the Reporter to the Children's Panel (Scottish system of dealing with juvenile offences)?
If yes
Was it for an offence?
Was drinking on *your* part involved in any way?
What was the outcome of the referral? Was action taken by the Reporter?
If yes
Were you discharged?
If not discharged
Were you given a supervision order with a social worker or supervision with a residential order?
If ever given supervision order, ask
 (i) Were you ever asked by a future employer if you had a conviction?
     Did you tell them about the supervision order?
(ii) Did you get the job?

65   In the past two years, have you ever been in trouble with the police?
If yes
Were you convicted?
If yes
How many times have you been convicted?
IF NEVER IN TROUBLE WITH POLICE, PROCEED TO Q.66

Otherwise ask

On the last occasion you were convicted (or 'in trouble') was your drinking involved?

If no

Did someone else say so?

[IF MORE THAN ONE CONVICTION, CODE FOR MOST RECENT, BUT **probe** FOR ASCRIPTION TO ALCOHOL IN OTHER CONVICTIONS AND RECORD BELOW,

e.g. 1979   Burglary (drunk)   6 months]

66   Have you been robbed or criminally assaulted in the past two years?

If yes

How many times has this happened?

67   (a) Does (did) your father (the male head of the household you grew up in) drink alcohol?

     If yes, ask

     Did (has) his drinking cause(d) any problems at work, in the family or with his health?

    (b) Does (did) your mother (the female head of the household you grew up in) drink alcohol?

     If yes, ask

     Did (has) her drinking cause(d) any problems at work, in the family or with her health?

    (c) **Ask all**

     Do (did) either of your parents (head of household) disapprove of your drinking?

68   Do you have any brothers or sisters over the age of 16? How many?

If any, ask

In your opinion, do any of them drink heavily?

Do any of them *never* drink?

69   Has any other member of your family, e.g. grandparent, aunt, uncle, cousin, ever had a drinking problem?

IF RESPONDENT HAS DRUNK IN PAST TWO YEARS, PROCEED TO Q.72. QS. 70 AND 71 ARE ONLY FOR RESPONDENTS WHO HAVE **not** DRUNK IN PAST TWO YEARS

70   I'm going to read you out a list of reasons why some people don't drink. Could you please tell me which reasons apply to you?

I don't like the taste
Drinking is unhealthy and makes you ill
Drinking costs too much
People who drink are wicked
Drinking is against my religion
Drinking makes people lose control of themselves
Drinking is evil
Once you start drinking you can't stop the habit
My parents disapprove strongly of anyone who drinks
Some other reason (please specify)

71   Do you think that you may start drinking one day?

Ask all respondents

72   Do you ever smoke tobacco?
      If no, PROCEED TO Q.73
      If yes, ask
      What do you mainly smoke?
      If 'rolls own' cigarettes or smokes a pipe, ask
      How much tobacco do you smoke in a week?
      If 'ready made' cigarettes smoked, ask
      How many cigarettes do you smoke per day?

73   **SHOWCARD C**   GIVE SHOWCARD TO RESPONDENT
      Read carefully through this list of drugs. Have you ever tried any
      of them for enjoyment or out of curiosity, but *NOT* for medicinal
      purposes?

      IF NEVER, PROCEED TO Q.74
      If yes, ASK RESPONDENT TO IDENTIFY WHICH DRUGS. THEN
      ASK, FOR EACH DRUG TAKEN:
           (i) Have you used it in the past six months?
           (ii) **If yes,** How often have you used it in past six months?

      (a) Cannabis (pot, marijuana, grass, hash, dope)
      (b) LSD (acid)
      (c) Barbiturates (barbs)
      (d) Mogadon
      (e) Librium
      (f) Valium
      (g) Glues, solvents, dry-cleaning fluids, fuels

    (h) Amphetamines (pep pills, speed)
    (i) Opium
    (j) Morphine (M)
    (k) Heroin (H, Horse)
    (l) Methadone
    (m) Cocaine
    (n) Sleeping-tablets/tranquillizers
    (o) PCP (Angel Dust)
    (p) Other (please specify)

For all past and present drug users, ask
Have you ever had any problems connected with your use of drugs in any of the following areas?

Financial	Work/School
Domestic	Legal
Social (outside home)	Health

If respondent reports using any kind of drug currently, ASK:
Would you find it hard or inconvenient to go without this drug/these drugs for a month?
If yes, ask
Would going without this drug/these drugs cause mild hardship or would it be a serious problem for you?

74   In the past two years, have you taken any of the above drugs at the same time as drinking?
If yes, ask How often?
Now I want to ask you a few more questions about your work situation and your hopes for the future.

75   How important to you is a job?
PROBE: Do you want a job at any cost? Or does it depend on a decent job? Perhaps you don't have much interest in having a job at all?

NOW CHOOSE ONLY ONE OF THE FOLLOWING:

Q.76. IS FOR THE CURRENTLY UNEMPLOYED/YOPS/OTHER GOVT SCHEMES AND INCLUDES MOTHERS/WIVES SEEKING WORK.

Q.77. IS FOR THE CURRENTLY EMPLOYED – FULL-TIME OR PART-TIME.

Q.78. IS FOR FULL-TIME STUDENTS.

QS.79 & 80. ARE FOR HOUSEWIVES/MOTHERS, NOT WORKING MORE THAN SEVEN HOURS OUTSIDE THE HOME AND NOT SEEKING MORE WORK.
And then proceed to Q.81

76 **Currently unemployed/YOPS/other Govt Schemes, Mothers/ Wives seeking work**

How long have you been out of work now?

Do you think that you will find a job in the next few months?

If yes, ask

Do you think it will be the kind of job you want?

How often do you spend time looking for a job?

If never

Can you explain why?

Are you bored during the day?

How many of your friends are unemployed?

What do you think is the most important reason for there being so much unemployment around?

And what do you think is the most important reason why you have no job?

77 **Employed, full- or part-time**

How many of your friends are unemployed now?

Of those who have jobs, would you say they are satisfied?

What do you think is the most important reason for there being so much unemployment around and so little job satisfaction?

Is your job the kind of work you hoped for when you were at school?

Are you satisfied with your present job?

If no, ask

What do you think is the most important reason why you haven't managed to find a satisfying job?

78 **Full-time students**

How many of your friends are either dissatisfied with their job, unemployed, or have little confidence of finding a good job after studies completed?

What do you think is the most important reason for there being so much unemployment, job dissatisfaction, and so little confidence for the future generally around?

When you finish your education, do you think you'll find a job?
If yes, ask
Do you think it will be the kind of job you want?
If believes it unlikely will find job or kind of job wanted, ask
What's your most important reason for thinking that?

79 **Housewife/mother, i.e. no more than seven hours' work outside home and not seeking work at present**
Do you think that you will ever want to work outside home on full- or part-time basis?
If yes
When will that be?
Do you think you will find a job?
Do you think it will be the kind of job you want?
If believes it unlikely will find job or kind of job wanted, ask
Why do you think your chances are poor? What's the main reason?

80 What were you doing before this (i.e. before taking on mother-hood, etc.)?
Did you think at that time that being a mother (or housewife) would be an improvement over what you were doing?
What do you think now? Is it an improvement?
Qs. 81 AND 82 ARE FOR RESPONDENTS WHO, AT ANY TIME, HAVE BEEN BOTH **employed and unemployed** SINCE LEAVING SCHOOL.
OTHERWISE PROCEED TO Q.83.

81 Do you drink more when you are out of work than in work?
IF RESPONDENT ANSWERS 'SAME' OR 'DON'T KNOW', PROCEED TO Q.82
If more, ask
Why do you think that is? Is it because of any of the following?

Drink raises my spirits
Drink gives me something to do and somewhere to be
Lot more time available
Easier to find drinking partners around when unemployed
The friends I have (had) when unemployed drink more than my friends at work

If less, ask
Why do you think you drink less when you are out of work? Is it because of any of the following?

Less money available
Do most of drinking with workmates during worktime
or after work
Don't feel sociable any more
Feel cut off from everybody – socially isolated
More pressure, from parents/friends, not to
drink, e.g. because no money

82   Do you spend more *time* drinking when you are out of work?
When you are out of work, do you take the same drinks, or do you
tend to try something else?
When you are out of work, do you tend to drink in the same places
as when you are in work?

83   Finally, I would like to take your full name and address again.
What is your date of birth?
Please write in the names and addresses of *two* relatives or close
friends through whom we could contact you in future if you move
from your present address.
How many times have you moved in the past two years?
Thank you very much for completing the interview. Here is a
letter giving a few details of what this study is for.

Appendix 3: Some Methodological Issues

This appendix is concerned with some aspects of the adequacy or dependability of the information collected during this follow-up study. These issues are important but are discussed as a postscript to the main part of this book which was concerned with changes noted between the first and third waves of data collection that were carried out in 1979/80 and 1983 respectively. This is not a comprehensive review of methodological issues. Only three main topics are considered. These are the reliability and validity of the data collected in the first two phases of the study and the influence upon the 1983 survey response of the sex of the interviewers.

RELIABILITY AND VALIDITY

The second wave of data collection was conducted as an exercise whereby the reliability (consistency) of the baseline data of this study could be gauged. A detailed comparison of these two data sets also permitted a limited assessment of the validity (truthfulness) of the results of the 1979/80 survey results that have been described in Chapter 3.

The initial wave of data collection was largely conducted before November, 1979. Twelve potential respondents were not, however, traced until February, 1980 when the first wave was completed. Fieldwork avoided the Christmas and New Year period when drinking patterns might have been extremely unusual. Some of the study group left school at the end of December, 1980. A second wave of fieldwork was conducted during March and April, 1981. This involved revisiting the five collaborating schools and repeating the original procedure with all of the original respondents who remained at school. Altogether 870 of the study group of 1,036 were found to be still at school and all of these individually completed questionnaires a second time. The instrument used during this phase of the study was the same as that employed in the first phase, except for the addition of one item. Details of this questionnaire are provided in Appendix 1.

Surveys of self-reported alcohol consumption are known to be affected by underreporting. According to some commentators this may be of serious magnitude, up to 70 per cent (e.g. Pernanen 1974; Midanik 1982a). The validity of survey data is extremely difficult to assess. Even so it was regarded as worth while to collect a second wave of data fairly soon after the beginning of this study for two reasons. Firstly this permitted an examination of the reliability of the initial data. Secondly this procedure, it was thought, might identify changes in the levels of exposure to alcohol education during the final few months of compulsory school attendance. Of these two reasons, the former was judged to be by far the more important since in a study of this type the adequacy of the information collected is a major consideration in survey research.

COMPARISON OF WAVES ONE AND TWO

For most of the study group at least three months had elapsed between their involvement in the two initial waves of the study. Even so it was not anticipated that drinking experiences would have been dramatically altered by the passage of a relatively short time, albeit a period which included Christmas and New Year. This view was broadly supported by comparing the overall results of data collected during the two initial phases of this study.

Overall Results

The levels of alcohol-related consequences reported by the study group were examined in relation to the 385 males and 485 females from whom information was collected during the second wave of fieldwork. Consistent with the passage of the 1980/81 festive season levels of self-reported experience of intoxication reported by both sexes rose slightly. Even so the general pattern of consequences reported by both sexes was virtually identical to that obtained during the initial wave of data collection.

As indicated by *Figures 3* and *4*, both males and females reported

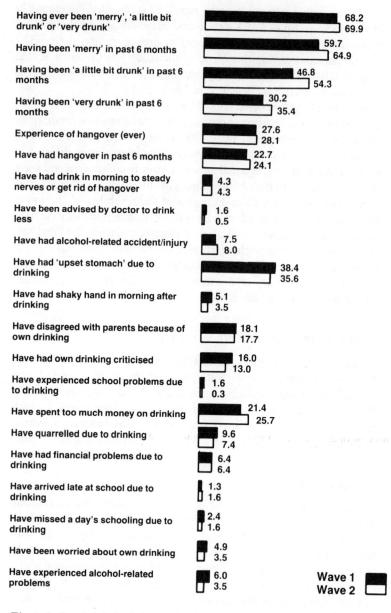

Having ever been 'merry', 'a little bit drunk' or 'very drunk' — 68.2 / 69.9

Having been 'merry' in past 6 months — 59.7 / 64.9

Having been 'a little bit drunk' in past 6 months — 46.8 / 54.3

Having been 'very drunk' in past 6 months — 30.2 / 35.4

Experience of hangover (ever) — 27.6 / 28.1

Have had hangover in past 6 months — 22.7 / 24.1

Have had drink in morning to steady nerves or get rid of hangover — 4.3 / 4.3

Have been advised by doctor to drink less — 1.6 / 0.5

Have had alcohol-related accident/injury — 7.5 / 8.0

Have had 'upset stomach' due to drinking — 38.4 / 35.6

Have had shaky hand in morning after drinking — 5.1 / 3.5

Have disagreed with parents because of own drinking — 18.1 / 17.7

Have had own drinking criticised — 16.0 / 13.0

Have experienced school problems due to drinking — 1.6 / 0.3

Have spent too much money on drinking — 21.4 / 25.7

Have quarrelled due to drinking — 9.6 / 7.4

Have had financial problems due to drinking — 6.4 / 6.4

Have arrived late at school due to drinking — 1.3 / 1.6

Have missed a day's schooling due to drinking — 2.4 / 1.6

Have been worried about own drinking — 4.9 / 3.5

Have experienced alcohol-related problems — 6.0 / 3.5

Wave 1
Wave 2

Figure 3. Levels of alcohol-related consequences reported by males during waves one and two (%)

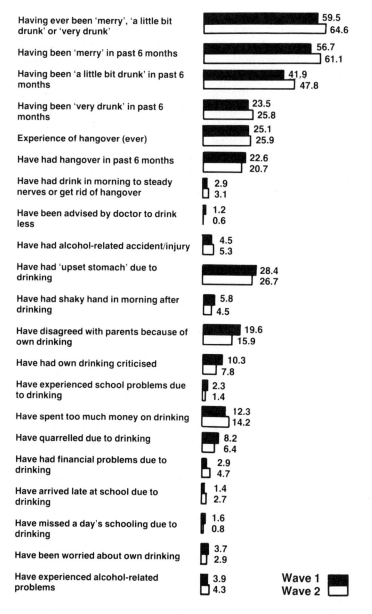

Figure 4. Levels of alcohol-related consequences reported by females during waves one and two (%)

similar levels of alcohol-related consequences during waves one and two. Apart from changes in intoxication experiences, only one consequence had altered by over 3 per cent amongst the males. This related to spending too much money on drink, which had risen by 4.3 per cent. Like intoxication, this change could have been explained by the passage of the festive season. Amongst females only one consequence apart from intoxication had altered by more than 3 per cent. This related to having disagreed with parents because of drinking. This was reported by 3.5 per cent *fewer* respondents during the second wave than during the first. This slight inconsistency may have been at least partly explained by the fact that some parents accepted drinking by their daughters more readily during the recent festive season than they had formerly.

Recollection of Alcohol Education

One reason for conducting the second wave of data collection was the possibility that respondents might receive alcohol education during their last year of compulsory attendance. In fact there was no significant change in the proportion of the 870 respondents who reported having received either information (48 per cent) or had seen a film (24 per cent) related to the use and misuse of alcohol.

The Consistency of Individual Responses

Figures 3 and *4* are reassuring. The *overall* pattern of alcohol-related consequences obtained during the first two waves of the study were very similar. A method of analysis which permitted assessment of consistency of *individual* responses was also used. This revealed a lower level of agreement. *Table 47* indicates the levels of correlation between

Table 47 Correlation between patterns of psychoactive drug use reported by the study group during waves one and two

measure of drug use	males	females
previous week's alcohol consumption	+0.5***	+0.4***
last occasion's alcohol consumption	+0.5***	+0.6***
number of cigarettes smoked each week	+0.8***	+0.9***
number of illicit drugs ever used	+0.5***	+0.6***

*** $p < 0.001$

patterns of psychoactive drug use reported by males and females during waves one and two.

As shown by *Table 47*, the correlations between these four drug measures ranged from +0.4 to +0.9. These levels are reasonably high, but indicate that alcohol consumption varied more between the two waves of data collection than did illicit drug use or smoking. The latter may have been the most consistent since even amongst teenagers, tobacco use frequently involved physical dependence which is seldom evident amongst teenage alcohol or illicit drug users

The levels of agreement were examined between alcohol-related consequences reported during waves one and two. A far from uniform pattern emerged. In relation to some items, such as the total number of alcohol-related consequences or the number of 'serious' consequences reported correlations exceeded +0.5. For most of the individual consequences (described in Chapter 3) lower correlations were evident.

Table 48 Percentage of respondents providing inconsistent answers in relation to their experience of alcohol-related consequences (waves one and two)

alcohol-related consequences*	male	female
have had an upset stomach due to drinking	13.2	10.5
have had own drinking criticized	9.9	5.6
have disagreed with parents about own drinking	8.6	10.7
experience of hangover	7.8	6.0
have quarrelled due to drinking	6.2	5.1
have been 'merry', 'a little bit drunk', or 'very drunk'	4.6	3.7
have experienced alcohol-related problems	4.2	2.1
have spent too much money on drinking	4.2	6.0
have been worried about own drinking	3.6	2.5
have had alcohol-related accident/injury	3.6	2.3
have had shaky hand in morning after drinking	3.1	3.9
have had financial problems due to drinking	3.1	1.2
have had drink in morning to steady nerves or get rid of hangover	2.3	2.1
have been advised by doctor to drink less	1.6	0.8
have experienced school problems due to drinking	1.3	1.2
have missed a day's schooling due to drinking	1.0	1.2
have arrived late at school due to drinking	0.5	0.4

*in rank order of frequency amongst males

Inconsistency

Some respondents gave contradictory replies. These individuals reported during the first wave of data collection that they had 'ever' experienced specific alcohol-related consequences. They then reported not ever having done so during the second phase of the study. Such inconsistencies may have been caused by error or by intention. The percentage of respondents who provided inconsistent answers to each of seventeen alcohol-related consequences is shown in *Table 48*.

The levels of inconsistency in reporting alcohol-related consequences ranged from 0.4 per cent to 13.2 per cent. More than 5 per cent of respondents of each sex provided inconsistent answers in relation to six of the seventeen consequences included in this table.

The relationship was examined between the total number of inconsistent answers provided by each respondent and their levels of self-reported alcohol use, alcohol-related consequences, and illicit drug use. Among both sexes inconsistency was significantly yet moderately associated with these measures. In addition inconsistency amongst males was also significantly but modestly associated with the number of serious alcohol-related consequences reported (significant correlations ranged from +0.2 to +0.3).

DISCUSSION

The two waves of data collection produced *overall* results that were very similar. In spite of this, individual consistency was low to medium in relation to many of the items compared. In fact some differences were to have been expected, since patterns of alcohol and other drug use are not static (e.g. Kandel 1978; Plant 1979a; Royal College of Physicians 1983; Edwards 1984). The two waves of data collection which are compared above covered a period (aged 15 to 17) when youthful experimentation with alcohol, tobacco, and illicit drugs may have been changing, or at least sporadic. There was far more variation in levels of alcohol use than in levels of weekly cigarette smoking, or in the number of illicit drugs used.

As shown in *Table 48*, a minority of the study group provided answers which were contradictory. These logical inconsistencies were associated, although only at a weak level, with general levels of self-reported alcohol, tobacco, and illicit drug use. Some of these anomalies may have been accidental. In addition they may have been caused by either overreporting during the first wave of the study and/or by underreporting during the second. The existence of these detectable inconsistencies suggests that other, undetected discrepancies may also have occurred. This type of anomaly would be indistinguishable from 'real changes' in respondents' experiences between the two initial phases of this study. For example some of the study group reported higher levels of intoxication during wave two than during wave one. Since Christmas and the New Year had occurred in the intervening period this is probably true.

Surveys of alcohol use are widely acknowledged to be afflicted by underreporting (Popham 1970; Schmidt 1972; Pernanen 1974; Midanik 1982a).

The link, though not strong, between inconsistency and self-reported levels of alcohol, tobacco, and illicit drug use, suggests that this study was biased not only by underreporting but also by over-reporting. This has been noted only seldom in relation to alcohol surveys (Midanik 1982b).

The two waves of data collection compared above revealed virtually identical pictures. The second wave in general terms reinforced the overall conclusions outlined in Chapter 3. Hidden amongst the general consistency, however, two far less reassuring pictures emerged. Firstly individual levels of uniformity were not high. Secondly some res-pondents were inconsistent and some of them may have intended to mislead. Together these conclusions provide a cautionary message about the interpretation of results from studies such as that described in this book. Surveys based upon self-reports may not be packs of lies. They provide a useful guide to interesting forms of behaviour, but almost certainly only a rough guide. One should not be tempted to place excessive trust in the precise percentages produced. It is worth keeping this advice in mind when considering the results of the third phase of this follow-up study. In addition it is emphasized that prospective surveys, though useful in many respects (Edwards 1984), provide only an imperfect way of examining processes and events which occur between discrete waves of data collection.

Validity of information refers to how far the measurements obtained measure what they are supposed to. Validity may be assessed in several ways. The most common of these is by comparison with similar infor-mation from an independent external source. Throughout this book the results of this study have been compared with those from other sources. It was reported, for example, in Chapters 3 to 9, that the patterns of alcohol, tobacco, and illicit drug use and misuse of the study group were similar to those noted in several British studies.

In Chapter 5 it was noted that the social-class background of the study group differed only very slightly from that of the overall population of the Lothian Region. The main ways in which the study group differed from expectations based upon other sources were the higher than expected percentage in full-time education and the lower than anticipated percentage who were married or unemployed. To some extent these differences may be related to social class bias.

The Effect of Interviewer's Sex on Response Patterns

It has been reported in earlier studies that self-reported survey data may be influenced by the sex of the interviewer (e.g. Cosper 1969). Efforts were made to arrange for the majority of respondents in this study to be interviewed during 1983 by a fieldworker of the same sex as themselves. Although this aim was achieved, a minority of respondents were interviewed by fieldworkers who were of the opposite sex to themselves.

There were too few males interviewed by females to permit a worthwhile analysis of this subgroup's responses. A comparison was, however, possible of the responses of females who were interviewed by males with responses of females who were interviewed by females. There were 451 female/female interviews and 58 female/male interviews. The results of this comparison are shown in *Table 49*.

It can be seen from *Table 49* that females who were interviewed by males were likely to admit drinking more alcohol and having used a

Table 49. Self-reported alcohol and illicit drug use by females who were interviewed by males and by females

psychoactive drug use	female interviewer	male interviewer
x̄ previous week's alcohol consumption (in units)*	6.3 (8.2)	9.5 (1.6)
x̄ number of illicit drugs ever used*	0.4 (0.9)	0.9 (2.0)
x̄ number of Category A drugs ever used*	0.04 (0.2)	0.14 (0.4)

figures in brackets are standard deviations
*significant

wider range of illicit drugs, including Category A drugs. The sex of the interviewer did not, however, produce significant differences in relation to levels of alcohol-related consequences and tobacco smoking, but even though these differences were not significant, they were consistently in the direction of females admitting to a higher level of 'deviant' behaviour when interviewed by males than when interviewed by females. It may seem possible to conclude that when a female is interviewed by a male she may feel less reluctance to admit to higher levels of alcohol and illicit drug consumption. Possibly this is because she considers that the male interviewer might also be a high consumer of these drugs. A female respondent is, however, equally reticent or open about admitting to alcohol-related consequences irrespective of the sex of the interviewer. It is worth emphasizing that a higher level of reporting may not be more valid than a lower level.

This result may be attributable to many factors. Possibly some interviewers were more skilled than others regardless of sex. Possibly females who were interviewed by males were those who were the hardest to follow up and therefore an atypical group. Irrespective of the reason for the differences that were evident, the possible interactions between the sex of the respondents and of the interviewers could usefully be explored further. What little evidence there is on this topic (e.g. Benny, Reisman, and Star 1956; Cosper 1969) suggests that the influence of interviewer characteristics on survey data is uncertain.

Bibliography

The following bibliography lists the main references that were useful in writing this book. Many, though not all, are referred to directly in the text.

Aaro, L. E., Bruland, E., Hauknes, A., and Lochsen, P. M. (1983) Smoking among Norwegian School Children 1975–1980. III. The Effect of Anti-Smoking Campaigns. *Scandinavian Journal of Psychology* 24: 1–7.

Abstract of Statistics (1975, 1981, 1984). London: Central Statistical Office.

Addiction Research Foundation (1982) *Statistics on Alcohol and Drug Use in Canada and Other Countries*. Toronto: Addiction Research Foundation.

Adlaf, E. M. and Smart, R. G. (1983) Risk-Taking and Drug Use Behaviour: An Examination. *Drug and Alcohol Dependence* 11: 287–96.

Adler, I. and Kandel, D. B. (1981) Cross-cultural Perspectives on Developmental Stages in Adolescent Drug Use. I. *Journal of Studies on Alcohol* 42, 9: 701–15.

Advisory Council on the Misuse of Drugs (1982) *Treatment and Rehabilitation*. London: Department of Health and Social Security.

—— (1984) *Prevention*. London: Home Office.

Ahlstrom, S. (1975) *Changing Drinking Habits among Finnish Youth. Report 81*. Helsinki: Social Research Institute of Alcohol Studies.

—— (1979) *Trends in Drinking Habits among Finnish Youth from the Beginning of the 1960's to the late 1970's. Report No. 128*. Helsinki: Social Research Institute of Alcohol Studies.

—— (1981) *Finnish Drinking Habits: A Review of Research and Trends in Acute Effects of Heavy Drinking. Report No. 150*. Helsinki: Social Research Institute of Alcohol Studies.

—— (1982a) *Finnish Teenagers – How They Drink and Clash with Authority. Report No. 159*. Helsinki: Social Research Institute of Alcohol Studies.

—— (1982b) *Pluralistic Ignorance and Finnish Young People's Estimates of Drinking. Report No. 165*. Helsinki: Social Research Institute of Alcohol Studies.

Aitken, P. P. (1978) *Ten-to-Fourteen Year Olds and Alcohol: A Developmental Study in the Central Region of Scotland (Vol. 3)*. Edinburgh: HMSO.

Aitken, P. P. and Jahoda, G. (1983) An Observational Study of Young Adults Drinking Groups. I. Drink Preferences, Demographic and Structural Variables as Predictors of Alcohol Consumption. *Alcohol and Alcoholism* 18, 2: 235–50.

Alderson, M. (1976) *An Introduction to Epidemiology*. London: Macmillan.

Anderson, D. (1979) *Health Education in Practice*. London: Croom Helm.

Armor, D., Polich, J., and Stambull, H. (1978) *Alcoholism and Treatment*. New York: Wiley.

Armyr, G., Elmer, A., and Herz, V. (1982) *Alcohol in the World of the 80's*. Stockholm: Sober Forlags A.G.

Ashton, H. and Stepnery, R. (1982) *Smoking – Psychology and Pharmacology*. London: Tavistock.

Ashton, M. (1984) Information supplied relating to the London Drug Indicators' Project (Institute for the Study of Drug Dependence). (Personal communication.)

Atkinson, J. M. (1978) *Discovering Suicide*. London: Macmillan.

Bachman, J. G., Johnston, L. D., and O'Malley, P. M. (1981) Smoking, Drinking and Drug Use among American High School Students: Correlates and Trends, 1975–1979. *American Journal of Public Health* 71, 1: 59–69.

Bacon, M. and Jones, M. B. (1968) *Teenage Drinking*. New York: Crowell Co.

Ball, J. C. (1967) The Reliability and Validity of Interview Data Obtained from 59 Narcotic Addicts. *American Journal of Sociology* 72: 650–54.

Bandy, P. and President, P. A. (1983) Recent Literature on Drug Abuse Prevention and Mass Media: Focussing on Youth, Parents, Women and the Elderly. *Journal of Drug Education* 13, 3: 255–71.

Banks, A. and Waller, T. A. N. (1983) *Drug Addiction and Polydrug Abuse*. London: Institute for the Study of Drug Dependence.

Barker, D. J. P. and Rose, G. (1984) *Epidemiology in Medical Practice*. Edinburgh: Churchill Livingstone.

Barnes, G. M. (1975) A Perspective on Drinking amongst Teenagers with Special Reference to New York State Studies. *Journal of School Health* 45, 7: 386–89.

Barry, H. B. (1974) Psychological Factors in Alcoholism. In B. Kissin and H. Bergleiter (eds) *The Biology of Alcoholism, 3*. New York: Plenum.

Bauman, K. E. and Bryan, E. S. (1980) Subjective Expected Utility and Children's Drinking. *Journal of Studies on Alcohol* 41, 9: 952–58.

Bauman, K. E., Koch, G. G., and Bryan, E. S. (1982) Validity of Self-Reports of Adolescent Cigarette Smoking. *International Journal of the Addictions* 17, 7: 1131–46.

Beaglehole, R., Brough, D., Harding, W., and Eyles, E. (1978) A Controlled Smoking Intervention Programme in Secondary Schools. *New Zealand Medical Journal* 87: 278–80.

Benny, M., Reisman, D., and Star, S. A. (1956) Age and Sex in the Interview. *American Journal of Sociology* 62: 143–52.

Berberian, R. M., Gross, C., Lovejoy, J., and Paparella, S. (1976) The Effectiveness of Drug Education: A Review. *Health Education Monographs* 4, 4: 377–98.

Berridge, V. and Edwards, G. (1981) *Opium and the People*. London: Allen Lane.

Biener, K. J. (1975) The Influence of Health Education on the Use of Alcohol and Tobacco in Adolescence. *Preventive Medicine* 4: 252–57.

Blane, H. T. (1979) Middle-aged Alcoholics and Young Drinkers. In H. T.

164   Alcohol, Drugs, and School-leavers

Blane and M. E. Chafetz (eds) *Youth, Alcohol and Social Policy*. New York: Plenum.

Blane, H. T. and Chafetz, M. E. (eds) (1979) *Youth, Alcohol and Social Policy*. New York: Plenum.

Blane, H. T. and Hewitt, L. E. (1977) *Alcohol and Youth: An Analysis of the Literature, 1960–1975*. Report for NIAAA. Contract ADM-281-75-0026. November.

Blaxter, M., Mullen, K., and Dyer, S. (1982) *Problems of Alcohol Abuse in the Western Isles: A Community Survey. Scottish Health Service Studies No. 44*. Edinburgh: Scottish Home and Health Department.

Boscarino, J. (1981) Predicting Drug Abuse from Social Demographic Factors: A Discriminant Function Analysis. *Addictive Behaviours* 6: 177–82.

Bostock, Y. and Davies, J. (1979) Recent Changes in the Prevalence of Cigarette Smoking in Scotland. *Health Bulletin* 37, 6: 260–67.

Brenner, M. H. (1972) *Mental Illness and the Economy*. Cambridge, Mass.: Harvard University Press.

—— (1975) Trends in Alcohol Consumption and Associated Illnesses. Some Effects of Economic Change. *American Journal of Public Health* 65: 1279–292.

—— (1979) Unemployment, Economic Growth and Mortality. *The Lancet*, 24 March, 672.

Brewers' Society (1982) *U.K. Statistical Handbook, 1981*. London: Brewers' Society.

—— (1983) *U.K. Statistical Handbook, 1982*. London: Brewers' Society.

—— (1984) *U.K. Statistical Handbook, 1983*. London: Brewers' Society.

Bruun, K. (1967) Drinking Patterns in Scandinavian Countries. *British Journal of Addiction* 62: 257–66.

Bruun, K., Edwards, G., Lumio, M., Makela, K., Pan, L., Popham, R. E., Room, R., Schmidt, W., Skog, O.-J., Sulkunen, P., and Osterberg, E. (1975) *Alcohol Control Policies in Public Health Perspective*. Helsinki: Finnish Foundation for Alcohol Studies.

Bruun, K., Pan, L., and Rexed, I. (1975) *The Gentleman's Club: International Control of Drugs and Alcohol*. Chicago: University of Chicago Press.

Burkett, S. R. and Carruthers, W. T. (1980) Adolescents' Drinking and Perceptions of Legal and Informal Sanctions: A Test of Four Hypotheses. *Journal of Studies on Alcohol* 41, 9: 839–53.

Burr, A. (1984) The Illicit Non-Pharmaceutical Heroin Market and Drug Scene in Kensington Market. *British Journal of Addiction* 79: 337–44.

Butler, J. T. (1982) Early Adolescent Alcohol Consumption and Self-Concept, Social Class and Knowledge of Alcohol. *Journal of Studies on Alcohol* 43, 5: 603–7.

Bynner, J. M. (1969) *The Young Smoker*. London: HMSO.

Caetano, R., Suzman, R. M., Rosen, D., and Voorhees-Rosen, D. J. (1982) The Shetland Islands: Drinking Patterns in the Community. *British Journal of Addiction* 77, 4: 415–31.

Cahalan, D. (1970) *Problem Drinkers: A National Survey*. San Francisco: Jossey-Bass.

Cahalan, D., Cisin, I. H., and Crossley, H. M. (1969) *American Drinking*

Practices. New Brunswick, NJ: Rutgers Center of Alcohol Studies. Monograph 6.

Cahalan, D. and Room, R. (1974) *Problem Drinking among American Men*. New Brunswick, NJ: Rutgers Center of Alcohol Studies. Monograph 7.

Cahalan, D. and Treiman, B. (1976) *Drinking Behavior, Attitudes and Problems in San Francisco*. Report prepared for Bureau of Alcoholism, Department of Public Health, City and County of San Francisco.

Camberwell Council on Alcoholism (1980) *Women and Alcohol*. London: Tavistock.

Cartwright, A. K. J., Shaw, S. J., and Spratley, T. A. (1978) The Relationship between Per Capita Consumption, Drinking Patterns and Alcohol-Related Problems in a Population Sample 1965–1974. Part 1. Increased Consumption and Changes in Drinking Patterns. *British Journal of Addiction* 73: 237–46.

Cashman, S. D. (1981) *Prohibition: The Lie of the Land*. New York: Free Press.

Casswell, S. (1983) Early Experiences with Alcohol: A Survey of an Eight and Nine Year Old Sample. *New Zealand Medical Journal* 96: 745, 1001–3.

Central Policy Review Staff (1979) *Alcohol Policies in the United Kingdom*. Stockholm: Sociologiska Institutionen, Stockholms Universitat. (Printed in 1982.)

City Roads (Crisis Intervention) and Phoenix House (1982) *Drug Resource Pack*. London: City Roads (Crisis Intervention Ltd) and Phoenix House.

Clark, J. P. and Tifft, L. (1966) Polygraph and Interview Validations of Self-Reported Deviant Behavior. *American Sociological Review* 31: 516–23.

Clark, W. B. (1976) Loss of Control, Heavy Drinking and Drinking Problems in a Longitudinal Setting. *Journal of Studies on Alcohol* 37: 1256–290.

Clark, W. B. and Cahalan, D. (1976) Changes in Problem Drinking over a Four Year Span. *Addictive Behaviours* 1: 251–59.

Clayson, C. (1972) *Report of Departmental Committee on Scottish Licensing Law*. London: HMSO.

Clegg, F. (1982) *Simple Statistics*. Cambridge: Cambridge University Press.

Cockett, R. (1971) *Drug Abuse and Personality in Young Offenders*. London: Butterworths.

Collins, J. J. (ed.) (1982) *Drinking and Crime*. London: Tavistock.

Cooke, D. J. and Allan, C. A. (1983) Self-Reported Alcohol Consumption and Dissimulation in a Scottish Urban Sample. *Journal on Studies on Alcohol* 4: 617–29.

Corder, B. W., Smith, R. A., and Swisher, J. D. (1975) *Drug Abuse Prevention*. Iowa: Wm. C. Brown Company Publishers.

Cosper, R. (1969) Interviewer Bias in a Study of Drinking Practices. *Quarterly Journal Studies on Alcohol* 30: 152–57.

Costello, R. M. (1975) Alcoholism Treatment and Evaluation: In Search of Methods. II. Collation of Two-Year Follow-up Studies. *International Journal of the Addictions* 10, 5: 857–67.

Cowley, J. C. P. (1977) Education about Alcohol – We Have Been this Way Before. *Royal Society Health Journal* 97, 1: 26–8.

Cox, A., Rutter, M., Yule, B., and Quinton D. (1977) Bias Resulting from Missing Information: Some Epidemiological Findings. *British Journal of Preventive and Social Medicine* 31: 131–36.

Crawford, A. (1984) Response Rates in British General Population Surveys of Alcohol Consumption: A Comparison. *Alcohol and Alcoholism* 19, 2: 141–45.

Crawford, A., Plant, M. A., Kreitman, N., and Latcham, R. (1984) Regional Variations in Alcohol-Related Morbidity in Britain: A Myth Uncovered? II. Population Survey. *British Medical Journal* 289: 1343–45.

Dale, J. J. (1978) An Evaluation of a Programme of School Health Education on Smoking. *Health Education Journal* 37, 11: 142–44.

Davies, J. B. (1980) Drinking and Alcohol-Related Problems in Five Industries. In B. D. Hore and M. A. Plant (eds) *Alcohol Problems in Employment*. London: Croom Helm.

Davies, J. B. and Stacey, B. (1972) *Teenagers and Alcohol: A Developmental Study in Glasgow (Vol. 2)*. London: HMSO.

Davies, P. T. (1982) The Pattern of Problems. In M. A. Plant (ed.) *Drinking and Problem Drinking*. London: Junction.

Davies, P. T. and Walsh, D. (1983) *Alcohol Problems and Alcohol Control in Europe*. London: Croom Helm.

de Haes, W. and Schuurman, J. (1975) Results of an Evaluation of Three Drug Education Methods. *International Journal of Health Education* XVIII, 4: 1–16.

de Lint, J. (1984) The Efficacy of Anti-Drink Propaganda. In N. Krasner, J. S. Madden, and R. J. Walker (eds) *Alcohol-Related Problems: Room for Manoeuvre*. Chichester: Wiley.

Department of Employment (1983) *Employment Gazette*. Table 2.15.

Department of the Environment (1970) *Drinking and Driving*. London: HMSO (Blennerhassett Committee).

Department of Health and Social Security (1981) *Drinking Sensibly*. London: HMSO.

Diccicio, L., Deutsch, C., Levine, G., Mills, D. J., and Unterberger, H. (1978) A School-Community Approach to Alcohol Education. *Health Education* 8: 11–13.

Dight, S. (1976) *Scottish Drinking Habits*. London: HMSO.

Ditecco, D. and Schlegl, P. (1982) Alcohol Use among Young Adult Males: An Application of Problem-Behavior Theory. In J. R. Eiser (ed.) *Social Psychology and Behavioral Medicine*. New York: Wiley.

Dobbs, J. and Marsh, A. (1983) *Smoking among Secondary School Children*. London: Office of Population Censuses and Surveys, Social Survey Division.

Doll, R. and Peto, R. (1976) Mortality in Relation to Smoking: 20 Years' Observations on British Male Doctors. *British Medical Journal* 4: 1525–536.

Donovan, J. E. and Jessor, R. (1978) Adolescent Problem Drinking: Psychosocial Correlates in a National Sample Study. *Journal of Studies on Alcohol* 39, 9: 1506–524.

Donovan, J. E., Jessor, R., and Jessor, L. (1983) Problem Drinking in Adolescence and Young Adulthood: A Follow-up Study. *Journal of Studies on Alcohol* 44, 1: 109–37.

Dorn, N. (1975/76) Notes on Prediction of Behavioural Change in Evaluation of Drug Education. *Drug and Alcohol Dependence* 1: 15–25.

—— (1980) There Ought to be a Law. *British Journal of Addiction* 75: 73–9.

—— (1981a) Social Analysis of Drugs in Health Education and the Media. In

G. Edwards and C. Busch (eds) *Drug Problems in Britain*. London: Academic Press.
—— (1981b) Youth Culture in the U.K.: Independence and Round Drinking. *International Journal of Health Education* XXIV, 2: 281–82.
—— (1983) *Alcohol, Youth and the State*. London: Croom Helm.
—— (1984) Never Mind the Width — What about the Quality? In N. Krasner, J. S. Madden, and R. J. Walker (eds) *Alcohol-Related Problems: Room for Manoeuvre*. Chichester: Wiley.
Downs, W. R. and Robertson, J. E. (1982) Adolescent Alcohol Consumption by Age and Sex of Respondent. *Journal of Studies on Alcohol* 43, 9: 1027–32.
Duffy, J. C. and Waterton, J. J. (1984) Under-Reporting of Alcohol Consumption in Sample Surveys: The Effect of Computer Interviewing in Field Work. *British Journal of Addiction* 79: 303–8.
Edwards, G. (1973) Epidemiology Applied to Alcoholism. *Quarterly Journal of Studies on Alcohol* 34: 28–56.
—— (1974) Drugs, Drug Dependence and the Concept of Plasticity. *Quarterly Journal of Studies on Alcohol* 35: 176–95.
—— (1982) *The Treatment of Drinking Problems*. London: Grant McIntyre.
—— (1984) Drinking in Longitudinal Perspective: Career and Natural History. *British Journal of Addiction* 79, 2: 175–84.
Edwards, G. and Busch, C. (eds) (1981) *Drug Problems in Britain*. London: Academic Press.
Edwards, G., Arif, A., and Jaffe, J. (eds) (1983) *Drug Use and Misuse: Cultural Perspectives*. Beckenham, Kent: Croom Helm.
Edwards, G. and Grant, M. (eds) (1977) *Alcoholism: New Knowledge and New Responses*. London: Croom Helm.
Edwards, G. and Littlejohn, J. (eds) (1984) *Pharmacological Treatments for Alcoholism*. London: Croom Helm.
Edwards, G., Chandler, J., and Hensman, C. (1972) Drinking in a London Suburb. *Quarterly Journal of Studies on Alcohol* 6: 69–93.
Endler, N. S. (1973) The Person versus Situation – a Pseudo Issue. A Response to Alker. *Journal of Personality* 41: 207–303.
Engs, R. (1978) College Students' Knowledge of Alcohol and Drinking. *Journal of the American College Health Association* 26: 189–93.
Erickson, P. G. (1982) Illicit Drug Use, Peer Attitudes and Perceptions of Harmful Effects among Convicted Cannabis Offenders. *International Journal of the Addictions* 17, 11: 141–54.
Erroll of Hale (1972) *Report of the Departmental Committee on Liquor Licensing*. London: HMSO.
Fagin, L. and Little, M. (1984) *The Forsaken Families*. Harmondsworth: Pelican.
Fazey, C. (1973) Merton, Retreatism and Drug Addiction: The Testing of a Theory. *Sociological Review* 21: 417–36.
—— (1977) *The Aetiology of Psychoactive Substance Use*. Paris: UNESCO.
Fillmore, K. M. (1974) Drinking and Problem Drinking in Early Adulthood and Middle Age: An Exploratory 20-Year Follow-up Study. *Quarterly Journal of Studies on Alcohol* 35: 819–40.
—— (1975) Relationships between Specific Drinking Problems in Early

168   Alcohol, Drugs, and School-leavers

Adulthood and Middle Age. *Journal of Studies on Alcohol* 36, 7: 882–907.

Finn, P. (1975) *Alcohol: You Can Help Your Kids to Cope.* New York: National Council on Alcoholism Inc.

—— (1977) Health Education and the Pleasures of Drinking. *Health Education* January/February 8, 1: 17–19.

—— (1977) Should Alcohol Education Be Taught with Drug Education? *Journal of School Health* 47, 8: 466–69.

—— (1978) The Development of Attitudinal Measures Toward Alcohol Education in the School and in the Home. *Journal of Drug Education* 8, 3: 203–19.

—— (1979) Alcohol Education in the School Curriculum. *Education and Prevention* 7, 8: 13–20.

—— (1979) Teenage Drunkenness: Warning Signal, Transient Boisterousness, or Symptoms of Social Change? *Adolescence* XIV 56: 819–34.

—— (1981) Institutionalizing Peer Education in the Health Education Classroom. *Journal of School Health* February: 91–5.

—— (1981) Teaching Students to be Lifelong Peer Educators. *Health Education* September/October: 13–16.

Finn, P. and Lawson, J. (1976) *Kids and Alcohol.* Washington, DC: US Government Printing Office.

Fishburne, P., Abelson, H., and Cisin, I. (1980) *The National Survey on Drug Abuse Main Findings 1979.* Washington, DC: US Government Printing Office.

Flatt, M. M. and Hills, D. R. (1968) Alcohol Abuse and Alcoholism in the Young. *British Journal of Addiction* 63: 183–91.

Flint, R. (1974) *Teenage Drinking: A Cause for Concern?* Edinburgh: Lothian Region Social Work Department.

Garretsen, H. F. L. and Knibbe, R. A. (1984) *Drinking Problems in the Netherlands: Intercorrelations and Relation with Consumption level.* Paper presented at Alcohol Epidemiology Symposium, ICAA, Edinburgh.

Gatherer, A., Parfit, J., Porter, E., and Vessey, M. (1979) *Is Health Education Effective?* Monograph No. 2. London: Health Education Council.

Gibbins, R., Israel, Y., Kalant, H., Popham, R. E., Schmidt, W., and Smart, R. G. (1974) *Research Advances in Alcohol and Drug Problems. Vol. One.* New York: Wiley.

Giesbrecht, N., Conroy, G., and Hobbs, M. (1984) *Level of Consumption and Alcohol-Related Problems: Preliminary Results from a Census of Males in Two Southern Ontario Communities.* Paper presented at Alcohol Epidemiology Symposium, ICAA, Edinburgh.

Gillies, P. A. and Wilcox, B. (1984) Reducing the Risk of Smoking amongst the Young. *Public Health* 98: 49–54.

Gillis, L. S. and Stone, G. L. (1977) The Fate of Drinkers: A 6-Year Follow-up Study of a Community Survey. *South African Medical Journal* 51: 789–91.

Globetti, G. (1971) Alcohol Education in the School. *Journal of Drug Education* 1, 3: 241–48.

Goldstein, M. S. (1975) Drinking and Alcoholism as Presented in College Health Textbooks. *Journal of Drug Education* 5: 109–23.

Gomberg, E. S. L. (1982) The Young Male Alcoholic. *Journal of Studies on Alcohol* 43, 7: 683–701.

Goode, E. (1970) *The Marijuana Smokers*. New York: Basic Books.
—— (1972) *Drugs in American Society*. New York: Alfred A. Knopf.
Goodstadt, M. S. (ed.) (1974) *Research on Methods of Drug Education*. Toronto: Addiction Research Foundation.
Goodstadt, M. S. (1974) *Myths and Methodology in Drug Education: A Critical Review of the Research Evidence*. Toronto: Addiction Research Foundation Substudy 588.
Goodstadt, M. S. and Sheppard, M. A. (1983) Three Approaches to Alcohol Education. *Journal of Studies on Alcohol* 44, 1: 362–80.
Goodstadt, M. S., Sheppard, M. A., and Chan, G. C. (1984) Non-Use and Cessation of Cannabis Use: Neglected Foci of Drug Education. *Addiction Behaviours* 9, 1: 21–32.
Gossop, M. (1982) *Living with Drugs*. London: Temple Smith.
Grant, M. (1979) Prevention. In M. Grant and P. D. V. Gwinner (eds) *Alcoholism in Perspective*. London: Croom Helm.
—— (ed.) (1980) *Alcohol Education for Young People in Scotland*. London: Alcohol Education Centre.
—— (1982a) Prevention. In M. A. Plant (ed.) *Drinking and Problem Drinking*. London: Junction, 163–88.
—— (1982b) *Young People and Alcohol Problems: Educating for Individual and Social Change*. Paper presented at 10th International Congress of the International Association for Child and Adolescent Psychiatry and Allied Professions, Dublin.
—— (1984a) The Moderating Influence: A Review of Trade-Sponsored Alcohol Education Programmes. *British Journal of Addiction* 79: 275–82.
—— (1984b) Planning Effective Alcohol Education. In N. Krasner, J. S. Madden, and R. J. Walker (eds) *Alcohol-Related Problems: Room for Manoeuvre*. Chichester: Wiley.
—— (1984c) *Same Again*. Harmondsworth: Pelican.
Grant, M. and Ritson, E. B. (eds) (1983) *Alcohol: The Prevention Debate*. London: Croom Helm.
Grant, M., Plant, M. A., and Williams, A. (eds) (1982) *Economics and Alcohol*. London: Croom Helm.
Greenblatt, M. and Schuckit, M. (eds) (1976) *Alcoholism Problems in Women and Children*. New York: Grune and Stratton.
Groves, W. E. (1974) Patterns of College Student Drug Use and Lifestyles. In E. Josephson and E. E. Carroll (eds) *Drug Use: Epidemiological and Sociological Approaches*. Washington, DC: Hemisphere.
Gusfield, J. R. (1981) *The Culture of Public Problems*. Chicago: University of Chicago Press.
Harbison, J. and Haire, T. (1980) *Drinking in Northern Ireland*. Belfast: Social Research Division, Public Policy Unit, Department of Finance.
Harford, T. C. (1981) *Environmental Influences in Adolescent Drinking*. Paper presented at 27th International Institute on the Prevention and Treatment of Alcoholism, ICAA, Vienna, Austria.
Harford, T. C. and Spiegler, D. L. (1983) Developmental Trends of Adolescent Drinking. *Journal of Studies on Alcohol* 44, 1: 181–87.
Harford, T. C., Wechsler, H., and Rohman, M. (1983) The Structural Context of College Drinking. *Journal of Studies on Alcohol* 44, 4: 722–32.

Harris, L. (1975) *Public Awareness of the National Institute on Alcohol Abuse and Alcoholism Advertising Campaign and Public Attitudes toward Drinking and Alcohol Abuse*. Overall study final report prepared for NIAAA. New York: Louis Harris and Associates.

Harrison, P. (1973) Young People and Drink. *New Society* 26, 586: 773–76.

Haskey, J. C., Balarajan, R., and Donnan, S. P. B. (1983) Regional Variations in Alcohol Related Problems within the United Kingdom. *Community Medicine* 5: 208–19.

Hassall, C. (1968) A Controlled Study of the Characteristics of Young Male Alcoholics. *British Journal of Addiction* 63: 203–8.

Hawker, A. (1978) *Adolescents and Alcohol*. London: Edsall.

Health Education Council (1983) *The Tyne Tees Alcohol Education Campaign: An Evaluation*. London: Health Education Council.

Heaney, S. (1984) An Evaluation of Alcohol Education in the School Setting. In N. Krasner, J. S. Madden and R. J. Walker (eds) *Alcohol-Related Problems: Room for Manoeuvre*. Chichester: Wiley.

Heather, N. and Robertson, I. (1981) *Controlled Drinking*. London: Methuen.

Hendry, L. B. (1983) *Growing Up and Going Out*. Aberdeen: Aberdeen University Press.

Hibell, B. (1981) *Trends in Drinking and Drug Habits in Swedish Youth from 1971 to 1980*. Paper presented to Alcohol Epidemiology Section of 27th International Institute on the Prevention and Treatment of Alcoholism, ICAA, Vienna, Austria.

Hingson, R., Heeren, T., Kovenock, D., Mangoine, T., Meyers, A., Morelock, S., Smith, R., Lederman, R., and Scotch, N. (1984) *Effects of Maine's 1981 and Massachusetts' 1982 Driving under the Influence Legislation*. Paper presented at Alcohol Epidemiology Symposium, ICAA, Edinburgh.

Hingson, R., Scotch, N., Day, N., and Culbert, A. (1980) Recognizing and Seeking Help for Drinking Problems. *Journal of Studies on Alcohol* 41: 1102–117.

Hingson, R., Scotch, N. A., Sorenson, J., and Swazey, J. P. (1981) *In Sickness and in Health*. St Louis: C. V. Mosby Company.

Hoinville, G., Jowell, R., and Associates (1982) *Survey Research Practice*. London: Heinemann.

Hollin, C. R. (1983) Young Offenders and Alcohol: A Survey of the Drinking Behaviour of a Borstal Population. *Journal of Adolescence* 6: 161–74.

Holmila, M., Partanen, J., Piispa, M., and Virtanen, M. (1980) *Alcohol Education and Alcohol Policy. Report No. 139*. Helsinki: Social Research Institute of Alcohol Studies.

Holtermann, S. and Burchell, A. (1981) *The Costs of Alcohol Misuse. Government Economic Service Working Paper No. 37*. London: Economic Advisor's Office, Department of Health and Social Security.

Home Office (1983) *Offences Relating to Motor Vehicles, England and Wales 1982*. Statistical Bulletin 21/83. London: Home Office.

—— (1983) *Statistics of the Misuse of Drugs in the U.K. in 1982*. London: Home Office.

—— (1984) *Statistics of the Misuse of Drugs in the U.K. 1983*. Statistical Bulletin. London: Home Office.

Hore, B. D. (1971) Life Events and Alcoholic Relapse. *British Journal of Addiction* 66: 83–8.

Hore, B. D. and Plant, M. A. (eds) (1980) *Alcohol Problems in Employment*. London: Croom Helm.

Hundleby, J. D. (1984) The Behavioural Framework of Adolescent Drug Use: Perspective Confirmation and Comparison of the Sexes. Paper presented at the University of Hamburg, 13 July.

Inciardi, J. A. (ed.) (1981) *The Drugs–Crime Connection*. Beverly Hills: Sage.

Institute for the Study of Drug Dependence (1982) *Drug Abuse Briefing*. London: Institute for the Study of Drug Dependence.

—— (1982) *Drugs in Health Education: Trends and Issues*. London: Institute for the Study of Drug Dependence.

—— (1982) *Facts and Feelings About Drugs: A Teachers' Manual*. London: Institute for the Study of Drug Dependence.

—— (1983) *Drug Link*. Spring, 1983. No. 18. London.

—— (1984) *Drug Link Information Letter*. 19, London: Institute for the Study of Drug Dependence.

—— (1984) *Drugs Demystified Training Pack*. London: Institute for the Study of Drug Dependence.

Jacobson, B. (1981) *The Lady Killers: Why Smoking Is a Feminist Issue*. London: Pluto.

Jahoda, G. and Crammond, J. (1972) *Children and Alcohol: A Developmental Study in Glasgow Vol. 1*. London: HMSO.

James, I. P. and d'Orban, P. J. (1970) Patterns of Delinquency among British Heroin Addicts. *Bulletin on Narcotics* 22: 13–19.

Jeffs, B. W. and Saunders, W. M. (1983) Minimizing Alcohol-Related Offences by Enforcement of the Existing Licensing Legislation. *British Journal of Addiction* 78: 67–78.

Jessor, R. and Jessor, S. L. (1975) Adolescent Development and the Onset of Drinking: A Longitudinal Study. *Journal of Studies on Alcohol* 36: 27–51.

—— (1978) Theory Testing in Longitudinal Research on Marihuana Use. In D. B. Kandel (ed). *Longitudinal Research on Drug Use*. New York: Halstead Press.

Jessor, R., Jessor, S. L., and Finney, J. A. (1983) A Social Psychology of Marihuana Use: Longitudinal Studies of High School and College Youth. *Journal of Personality and Social Psychology* 26: 1–15.

Johnson, B. D. (1973) *Marihuana Users and Drug Subcultures*. New York: Wiley.

Johnson, B. D., Bachman, J. E., and O'Malley, P. M. (1980) *Monitoring the Future. Questionnaire Responses from the Nation's High School Seniors 1979*. Ann Arbor, Mich.: Survey Research Center, University of Michigan.

Johnson, L. D. (1974) Drug Use During and After High School: Results of a National Longitudinal Study. *American Journal of Public Health* 64 (Suppl.): 29–37.

Johnson, R. F. Q. (1976) Pitfalls in Research: The Interview as an Illustrative Model. *Psychological Reports* 38: 3–17.

Josephson, E. and Rosen, M. (1978) Panel Loss in a High School Drug Study. In D. B. Kandel (ed.) *Longitudinal Research on Drug Use*. New York: Wiley.

Kalant, O. J. (ed.) (1980) *Research Advances in Alcohol and Drug Problems. Volume 5: Alcohol and Drug Problems in Women.* New York: Plenum.

Kalb, M. (1975) The Myth of Alcoholism Prevention. *Preventative Medicine* 4: 404–16.

Kallen, D. B. P., Kosse, G. B., Wagenaar, H. C., Klaprogge, J. J. J., and Vorbeck, M. (eds) (1982) *Social Science Research and Public Policy-Making: A Reappraisal.* Windsor: NFER-Nelson.

Kandel, D. B. (ed.) (1978) *Longitudinal Research on Drug Use.* New York: Halstead.

—— (1980) Drug and Drinking Behaviour among Youth. *Annual Review of Sociology* 6: 235–85.

—— (1982) Epidemiological and Psychosocial Perspectives on Adolescent Drug Use. *Journal of the American Academy of Child Psychiatry* 21, 4: 328–47.

Kandel, D. B., Single, E., and Kessler, R. C. (1976) The Epidemiology of Drug Use among New York State High School Students: Distribution, Trends and Changes in Rates of Use. *American Journal of Public Health* 66: 43–53.

Kasl, S. V. (1979) Mortality and the Business Cycle: Some Questions about Research Strategies when Utilizing Macro-ecological Data. *American Journal of Public Health* 69, 8: 784–88.

Kellam, S. G., Ensminger, M. E., and Turner, R. J. (1977) Family Structure and the Mental Health of Children. *Archives of General Psychiatry* 34: 1012–22.

Kendell, R. E. (1979) Alcoholism: A Medical or a Political Problem. *British Medical Journal*: 367–71.

Kendell, R. E., de Roumanie, M., and Ritson, E. B. (1983) Effect of Economic Changes on Scottish Drinking Habits. *British Journal of Addiction* 78: 365–80.

Kilich, S. and Plant, M. A. (1981) Regional Variations in Levels of Alcohol-Related Problems in Britain. *British Journal of Addiction* 76: 47–62. Also erratum note 1982: 77, 211.

Kinder, B. N., Pape, N. E., and Walfish, S. (1980) Drug and Alcohol Education Programmes: A Review of Outcome Studies. *International Journal of the Addictions* 15: 1035–54.

Knight, I. and Wilson, P. (1980) *Scottish Licensing Laws.* London: HMSO.

Knistern, J., Biglan, A., Lichtenstein, E., Ary, D., and Bavry, J. (1983) Peer Modelling Effects in the Smoking Behaviour of Teenagers. *Addictive Behaviours* 8: 129–32.

Knupfer, G. (1967) The Epidemiology of Problem Drinking. *American Journal of Public Health* 57, 6: 973–86.

—— (1984) The Risks of Drunkenness. *British Journal of Addiction* 79: 185–96.

Kohn, P. M., Smart, R. G., and Ogborne, A. C. (1984) Effects of Two Kinds of Alcohol Advertising on Subsequent Consumption. *Journal of Advertising* 13, 1: 34–48.

Krasner, N., Madden, J. S., and Walker, R. J. (eds) (1984) *Alcohol-Related Problems: Room for Manoeuvre.* Chichester: Wiley.

Kreitman, N. (1977) Three Themes in the Epidemiology of Alcoholism. In G. Edwards and M. Grant (eds) *Alcoholism: New Knowledge and New Perspectives.* London: Croom Helm.

—— (1982) The Perils of Abstention? *British Medical Journal* 284: 444.

Langone, J. (1976) *Bombed, Buzzed, Smashed or Sober: A Book about Alcohol.* New York: Avon.

Latcham, R. (1984) (Personal communication).

Latcham, R., Kreitman, N., Plant, M. A., and Crawford, A. (1984) Regional Variations in Alcohol-Related Morbidity in Britain: A Myth Uncovered? I. Clinical Surveys. *British Medical Journal* 289: 1341–343.

Ledwith, F. (1983) A Study of Smoking in Primary and Secondary Schools in Lothian Region. (Personal communication.)

Liban, C. and Smart, R. G. (1980) Generational and Other Differences between Males and Females in Problem Drinking and its Treatment. *Drug and Alcohol Dependence* 5: 207–21.

Lloyd, D. M., Alexander, H. M., Callcott, R., Dobson, A. J., Hardes, G. R., O'Connell, D. L., and Leeder, S. R. (1983) Cigarette Smoking and Drug Use in School Children. III. Evaluation of a Smoking Prevention Education Programme. *International Journal of Epidemiology* 12, 1: 51–58.

Lonsdale, C. J. and Stacey, B. G. (1981) *An Analysis of Drink-Driving Research in New Zealand.* Christchurch: Psychology Department, University of Canterbury.

Lourie, R. S. (1943) Alcoholism in Children. *American Journal of Orthopsychiatry* 13: 322–38.

Lucas, W. L., Grupp, S. E., and Schmitt, R. L. (1975) Predicting Who Will Turn on: A Four-Year Follow-up. *International Journal of the Addictions* 10: 305–26.

McAlister, A., Perry, C., Killen, J., Slinkard, L. A., and Maudsy, N. (1980) Pilot Study of Smoking, Alcohol and Drug Abuse Prevention. *American Journal of Public Health* 70, 7: 719–25.

MacAndrew, C. and Edgerton, R. B. (1970) *Drunken Comportment: A Social Explanation.* London: Nelson.

McClelland, D. C., Davis, W. N., and Kahn, R. (1972) *The Drinking Man.* New York: Free Press.

McCord, W. and McCord, J. (1959) *Origins of Crime.* New York: Columbia University Press.

—— (1960) *Origins of Alcoholism.* Stanford: Stanford University Press.

—— (1962) A Longitudinal Study of the Personality of Alcoholics. In D. J. Pittman and C. R. Snyder (eds) *Society, Culture and Drinking Patterns.* New York: Wiley.

McGrath, J. H. and Scarpitti, F. R. (1970) *Youth and Drugs.* Glenview, Ill.: Scott, Foreman and Co.

McGuffin, S. J. (1980) Patterns of Drinking in Northern Ireland Young People. Paper presented at British Psychological Society meeting, Belfast, 11 December.

McKechnie, R. J., Cameron, D., Cameron, I. A., and Drewery, J. (1977) Teenage Drinking in South-West Scotland. *British Journal of Addiction* 72: 287–95.

Maddox, G. L. (1962) Teenage Drinking in the United States. In D. J. Pittman and C. R. Snyder (eds) *Society, Culture and Drinking Patterns.* New York: Wiley.

174   Alcohol, Drugs, and School-leavers

—— (1966) Teenagers and Alcohol: Recent Research. *Annals of the New York Academy of Science* 133: 856–65.

Maddox, G. L. and McCall, B. C. (1964) *Drinking among Teenagers*. New Brunswick, NJ: Rutgers Center on Alcohol Studies.

Makela, K. (1975) *Notes on the Relationship between Alcohol Problems*. Helsinki: Research Institute of Alcohol Studies.

—— (1982) *Permissible Starting Age for Drinking in Four Scandinavian Countries*. Oslo: Statens Institute for Alkoholforskning.

Makela, K., Room, R., Single, E., Sulkunen, P., and Walsh, B. (eds) (1981) *Alcohol, Society and the State 1: A Comparative Study of Alcohol Control*. Toronto: Addiction Research Foundation.

Manpower Services Commission (1984a) *Labour Market Quarterly Report (Scotland)*. August: 4.

—— (1984b) (Personal communication).

Margulies, R. Z., Kessler, R. C., and Kandel, D. B. (1977) A Longitudinal Study of Onset of Drinking among High School Students. *Journal of Studies on Alcohol* 38: 897–912.

Market and Opinion Research International (1981) *The Effects of Advertising on Alcohol Consumption*. London: Market and Opinion Research International.

Marsh, A. and Matheson, J. (1983) *Smoking Attitudes and Behaviour*. London: Office of Population Censuses and Surveys, Social Survey Division.

Marsh, C. (1982) *The Survey Method*. London: George Allen & Unwin.

Mayer, J. E. and Filstead, W. J. (eds) (1980) *Adolescence and Alcohol*. Cambridge, Mass.: Ballinger.

Medical Research Council (1983) *Annual Report April 1982–March 1983*. London: Medical Research Council.

Mednick, S. A. and Baert, A. E. (eds) (1981) *Prospective Longitudinal Research*. Oxford: Oxford University Press.

Mellinger, G. D., Somers, R. H., and Manheimer, D. I. (1975) Drug Use Research Items Pertaining to Personality and Interpersonal Relations: A Working Paper for Research Investigators. In D. J. Lettieri (ed.) *Predicting Adolescent Drug Abuse: A Review of Issues, Methods and Correlates*. National Institute of Drug Abuse, Washington, DC: US Government Printing Office.

Melville, A. and Johnson, C. (1982) *Cured to Death*. London: Secker & Warburg.

Merrill, E. (1978) *Glue-Sniffing*. Birmingham: PEPAR Publications.

Midanik, L. (1982a) The Validity of Self-Reported Alcohol Consumption and Alcohol Problems: A Literature Review. *British Journal of Addiction* 77, 4: 357–82.

—— (1982b) Over Reports of Recent Alcohol Consumption in a Clinical Population: A Validity Study. *Drug and Alcohol Dependence* 9: 101–10.

—— (1983) Familial Alcoholism and Problem Drinking in a National Drinking Practices Survey. *Addictive Behaviours* 8: 133–41.

Milgram, G. G. (1974) Alcohol Education in the Schools Perceived by Educators and Students. *Journal of Alcohol and Drug Education* 20, 1: 4–12.

—— (1979) *Alcohol Education Materials*. New Brunswick, NJ: Rutgers Center of Alcohol Studies.

Miller, K. D., Williams, A. F., and Heller, J. (1981) Blood Alcohol

Concentrations of Patrons Leaving a College Pub. *Journal of Studies on Alcohol* 42, 7: 676–79.

Mills, K. C., Neal, E. M., and Peed-Neal, I. (1983) *Handbook for Alcohol Education*. Cambridge, Mass.: Ballinger.

Minford, P. C. (1983) *Unemployment: Cause and Cure*. Oxford: Martin Robertson.

Mischel, W. (1969) Continuity and Change in Personality. *American Psychologist* 24: 1012–18.

Moberg, D. P. (1983) Identifying Adolescents with Alcohol Problems: A Field Test of the Adolescent Alcohol Involvement Scale, *Journal of Studies on Alcohol* 44, 4: 701–21.

Moore, M. H. and Gerstein, D. R. (eds) (1981) *Alcohol and Public Policy*. Washington, DC: National Academy Press.

Morgan, P. A. (1979) *Youthful Drinking in San Francisco*. Final report for California Department of Alcohol and Drug Abuse.

MORI Led. (1980) Opinion poll conducted for *Sunday Times* (London). Quota survey of 1,058 respondents carried out in 53 British constituencies.

Moser, J. (1979) *Prevention of Alcohol-Related Problems*. Geneva: World Health Organisation.

—— (1980) *Prevention of Alcohol-Related Problems*. Toronto: World Health Organisation, Addiction Research Foundation.

Mosher, J. F. (1981) The History of Youthful Drinking Laws: Implications for Current Policy. (Personal communication.)

Moss, M. C. and Davies, E. B. (1967) *A Survey of Alcoholism in an English County*. London: Geigy.

Mott, J. (1985) Self-reported Cannabis Use in Great Britain in 1981. *British Journal of Addiction* 80: 37–44.

Mules, J. E., Hague, W. H., and Dudley, D. L. (1977) Life Change, its Perception and Alcohol Addiction. *Journal of Studies on Alcohol* 38: 487–93.

Murray, M., Swan, A. V., Enock, C., Johnson, M. R. D., Banks, M. H., and Reid, D. J. (1982) The Effectiveness of the Health Education Council's 'My Body' School Health Education Project. *Health Education Journal* 41, 4: 126–30.

Murray, R., Ghodse, H., Harris, C., Williams, D., and Williams, P. (eds) (1981) *The Misuse of Psychotropic Drugs*. Special Publication 1. London: Gaskell.

Myers, T. (1982) *Drinking and Driving: Notes on the Relationship with a Focus on Scotland*. (Personal communication.)

NOP Market Research Ltd (1982) Survey of drug use in the 15–21 age group undertaken for the *Daily Mail*. NOP, London.

North, R. and Orange, R., Jnr (1980) *Teenage Drinking: The Number One Drug Threat to Young People Today*. New York: Collier.

O'Connor, J. (1978) *The Young Drinkers*. London: Tavistock.

—— (1984) Models of Drinking Behaviour and their Implications for Health Education of the Young. In N. Krasner, J. S. Madden, and R. J. Walker (eds) *Alcohol-Related Problems: Room for Manoeuvre*. Chichester: Wiley.

O'Donohue, N. and Richardson, S. (eds) (1984) *Pure Murder: A Book about Drug Use*. Dublin: Women's Community Press.

176   Alcohol, Drugs, and School-leavers

Office of Population Censuses and Surveys (1980) *General Household Survey 1978*. London: HMSO.
—— (1983) *General Household Survey: Cigarette Smoking 1972–1982*. London: HMSO.
—— (1984) *General Household Survey 1982*. London: HMSO.
Ojesjo, L. (1981) Long-term Outcome in Alcohol Abuse and Alcoholism amongst Males in the Lundby General Population, Sweden. *British Journal of Addiction* 76, 4: 391–400.
Ojesjo, L., Hagnell, O., and Lanke, J. (1982) Incidence of Alcoholism among Men in the Lundby Community Cohort, Sweden, 1957–1972. *Journal of Studies on Alcohol* 43, 11: 1190–98.
Orford, J. and Edwards, G. (1977) *Alcoholism*. New York: Oxford University Press.
Orford, J. and Harwin, J. (eds) (1982) *Alcohol and the Family*. London: Croom Helm.
Pandina, R. J. and Schuele, J. A. (1983) Psychosocial Correlates of Alcohol and Drug Use of Adolescent Students and Adolescents in Treatment. *Journal of Studies on Alcohol* 44, 6: 950–73.
Pandina, R. J. and White, H. R. (1981) Patterns of Alcohol and Drug Use of Adolescent Students and Adolescents in Treatment. *Journal of Studies on Alcohol* 42, 5: 441–56.
Peck, D. F. (1982) Some Determining Factors. In M. A. Plant (ed.) *Drinking and Problem Drinking*. London: Junction/Fourth Estate.
Pernanen, K. (1974) Validity of Survey Data on Alcohol Use. In R. J. Gibbins, Y. Israel, H. Kalant, R. E. Popham, W. Schmidt, and R. G. Smart (eds) *Research Advances in Alcohol and Drug Problems. Vol. 1*. New York: John Wiley.
Perry, C., Telch, M. J., Killen, J., Burke, A., and Maccoby, N. (1983) High School Smoking Prevention: The Relative Efficacy of Varied Treatments and Instructions. *Adolescence* XVIII, 71: 561–66.
Peterson, D. R. (1968) *Clinical Study of Social Behaviour*. New York: Appleton, Century, Crofts.
Pittman, D. J. (1980) *Primary Prevention of Alcohol Abuse and Alcoholism*. St Louis: Social Science Institute, Washington University.
Pittman, D. J. and Snyder, C. R. (1962) *Society, Culture and Drinking Patterns*. New York: Wiley.
Plant, M. A. (1975) *Drugtakers in an English Town*. London: Tavistock.
—— (1979a) *Drinking Careers*. London: Tavistock.
—— (1979b) Estimating Drinking Patterns and the Prevalence of Alcohol-Related Problems. *British Journal on Alcohol and Alcoholism* 14: 132–39.
—— (1980) Drug Taking and Prevention: The Implications of Research for Social Policy. *British Journal of Addiction* 75: 245–54.
—— (1981a) *Drugs in Perspective*. London: Hodder and Stoughton.
—— (1981b) What Aetiologies? In G. Edwards and C. Busch (eds) *Drug Problems in Britain*. London: Academic Press.
—— (ed) (1982) *Drinking and Problem Drinking*. London: Junction.
—— (1984) Alcohol in Britain: Patterns, Problems, Paradoxes and Public

Policy. In E. Single and T. Storm (eds) *Public Drinking and Public Policy.* Toronto: Addiction Research Foundation.

—— (1985) The Epidemiology of Alcohol Use and Misuse. *Medicine* (in press).

Plant, M. A. and Miller, T. I. (1977) Disguised and Undisguised Questionnaires Compared: Two Alternative Approaches to Drinking Behaviour Surveys. *Social Psychiatry* 12: 21–4.

Plant, M. A., Peck, D. F., Samuel, E., and Stuart, R. (1985) The Reliability and Validity of Self-Reported Alcohol Consumption and Alcohol-Related Consequences amongst Scottish Teenagers. *Drinking and Drug Practices Surveyor* (in press).

Plant, M. A., Peck, D. F., and Stuart, R. (1982) Self-Reported Drinking Habits and Alcohol-Related Consequences amongst a Cohort of Scottish Teenagers. *British Journal of Addiction* 77: 75–90.

Plant, M. A., Peck, D. F., and Stuart, R. (1984) The Correlates of Serious Alcohol-Related Consequences and Illicit Drug Use amongst a Cohort of Scottish Teenagers. *British Journal of Addiction* 79, 2: 197–200.

Plant, M. A. and Pirie, F. (1979) Self-Reported Alcohol Consumption and Alcohol-Related Problems: A Study in Four Scottish Towns. *Social Psychiatry* 14: 65–73.

Plant, M. A., Pirie, F., and Kreitman, N. (1979) Evaluation of the Scottish Health Education Unit's 1976 Campaign on Alcoholism. *Social Psychiatry* 14: 11–24.

Plant, M. L. (1985) *Women, Drinking and Pregnancy.* London: Tavistock.

Plant, M. L. and Plant, M. A. (1979) Self-Reported Alcohol Consumption and Other Characteristics of 100 Patients Attending a Scottish Alcoholism Treatment Unit. *British Journal on Alcohol and Alcoholism* 14: 197–207.

Platt, S. and Kreitman N. (1984) Trends in Parasuicide and Unemployment among Edinburgh Men, 1968–1982. *British Medical Journal* (in press).

Polich, J. M. (1979) Alcohol Problems among Civilian and Military Youth. In H. T. Blane and M. E. Chaftetz (eds) *Youth, Alcohol and Social Policy.* New York: Plenum.

Polich, J., Armor, D., and Braiker, H. (1981) *The Course of Alcoholism: 4 Years After Treatment.* New York: Wiley.

Popham, R. E. (1970) Indirect Methods of Alcoholism Prevalence Estimation: A Critical Review. In R. E. Popham (ed.) *Alcohol and Alcoholism.* Toronto: Toronto University Press.

Rachel, J. V., Hubbard, R. L., Williams, J. R. (1976) Drinking Levels and Problem Drinking among Junior and Senior High School Students. *Journal of Studies on Alcohol* 37: 1751–61.

Rachel, J. V., Maisto, S. A., Guess, L. L., and Hubbard, R. L. (1980) *Use and Misuse of Alcohol by United States Adolescents – Recent Information from Two National Surveys.* Paper presented at 26th International Institute on the Prevention and Treatment of Alcoholism, ICAA, Cardiff.

Radosevich, M., Lanza-Kaduce, L., Akers, R. L., and Krohn, M. D. (1979) The Sociology of Adolescent Drug and Drinking Behaviour: A Review of the State of the Field: Part I. *Deviant Behaviour* : 15–35.

Raison, T. (ed.) (1966) *Youth in New Society.* London: Rupert Hart-Davis.

178   Alcohol, Drugs, and School-leavers

Randall, D. and Wong, M. R. (1976) Drug Education to Date: A Review. *Journal of Drug Education* C. 1: 1–21.

Ratcliff, K. E. and Burkhart, B. R. (1984) Sex Differences in Motivations for and Effects of Drinking among College Students. *Journal of Studies on Alcohol* 45, 1: 26–33.

Regional Working Party on Problem Drinking (1983) *Drinking Problems?* Newcastle: North East Council on Alcoholism.

Registrar General Scotland (1982) *Census 1981 Scotland. Report for Lothian Region. Volume 1.* Edinburgh: HMSO.

Reiskin, H. W. and Wechster, H. (1981) Drinking among College Students Using a Campus Mental Health Center. *Journal of Studies on Alcohol* 42, 9: 716–24.

Release (1982) *Trouble with Tranquillisers.* London: Release Publications, Ltd.

Richardson, R. G. (ed.) (1971) *The Second Work Conference on Smoking and Health.* London: Pitman Medical.

Robertson, J. R. (1985) Drug Users in Contact with General Practice. *British Medical Journal* 290: 31–2.

Robins, L. N. (1966) *Deviant Children Grown Up.* Baltimore: Williams & Wilkins.

—— (1974) *The Vietnam Drug User Returns* (Final Report, Special Action Office, Monograph, Series A. No. 2). Washington, DC: Government Printing Office.

—— (1975) Veterans' Drug Use Three Years After Vietnam. Unpublished manuscript cited by Josephson and Rosen (1978).

—— (1978) The Interaction of Setting and Predisposition after Vietnam. In D. B. Kandel (ed.) *Longitudinal Research on Drug Use.* New York: Halstead, 179–98.

Robins, L. N., Davis, D. H., and Nivco, D. N. (1974) How Permanent Was Vietnam Drug Addiction? *American Journal of Public Health* 64 (Suppl.): 38–43.

Roizen, R., Cahalan, D., and Shanks, P. C. (1978) 'Spontaneous Remission' among Untreated Problem Drinkers. In D. B. Kandel (ed.) *Longitudinal Research on Drug Use.* New York: Halstead.

Room, R. (1972) Drinking Patterns in Large U.S. Cities: A Comparison of San Francisco and National Samples. *Quarterly Journal of Studies on Alcohol*, Suppl. 6: 28–57.

—— (1978) Alcohol in Casualties and Crime: The Current State of Research and Future Directions. Paper presented at 24th International Institute on the Prevention and Treatment of Alcoholism, ICAA, Zurich.

—— (1984) The World Health Organisation and Alcohol Control. *British Journal of Addiction* 79, 1: 85–92.

Rooney, J. F. (1982) Perceived Differences of Standards for Alcohol Use among American Youth. *Journal of Studies on Alcohol* 43, 11: 1069–83.

Rootman, I. and Hughes, P. H. (1980) *Drug-Abuse Reporting Systems.* Offset Publications No. 55. Geneva: World Health Organisation.

Rorstad, P. (1984) (Personal communication).

Rosenburg, C. M. (1969) Young Alcoholics. *British Journal of Psychiatry* 115: 181–88.

Rosner, A. C. (1975) Drug and Alcohol Abuse Education: Opinions of School Principals. *Journal of School Health* 45: 568–69.

Ross, H. L. (1984) *Deterring the Drinking Driver*. Lexington, Mass.: Lexington Books.

Rowntree, D. (1981) *Statistics without Tears*. Harmondsworth: Pelican.

Royal College of Physicians (1983) *Health or Smoking?* London: Pitman.

Royal College of Psychiatrists (1979) *Alcohol and Alcoholism*. London: Tavistock.

Rutledge, B. and Fulton, E. K. (eds) (1977) *International Collaboration: Problems and Opportunities*. Toronto: World Health Organisation, Addiction Research Foundation.

Sabey, B. E. and Staughton, G. C. (1980) *The Drinking Road-User in Great Britain*, Transport and Road Laboratory, Supplementary Report 616, Berkshire, Department of the Environment, Department of Transport.

Samuel, E. (1984) Alcohol Education in Schools: Assessing the Scope for Constraints Upon New Initiatives. Paper presented at Alcohol Epidemiology Symposium, ICAA, Edinburgh.

Sargent, M. (1979) *Drinking and Alcoholism in Australia*. Melbourne: Longman.

Saunders, W. M. and Kershaw, P. W. (1978) The Prevalence of Problem Drinking and Alcoholism in the West of Scotland. *British Journal of Psychiatry* 13: 493–99.

—— (1979) Spontaneous Remission from Alcoholism — a Community Study. *British Journal of Addiction* 74: 251–54.

Schaps, E., Dibartolo, R., Moskowitz, J., Balley, C. G., and Churgin, G. (1981) A Review of 127 Drug Abuse Prevention Programme Evaluations. *Journal of Drug Issues* 11, 1: 17–43.

Schilder, P. (1941) The Psychogenesis of Alcoholism. *Quarterly Journal of Studies on Alcohol* 2: 277–92.

Schmidt, D. W. (1972) *Analysis of Alcohol Consumption Data: The Use of Consumption Data for Research Purposes. Report on the Conference on Epidemiology of Drug Dependence*. London: World Health Organisation.

Schneiderman, I. (1975) Family Thinking in Prevention of Alcoholism. *Preventive Medicine* 4: 296–309.

Schulsinger, F., Mednick, S. A., and Knop, J. (eds) (1982) *Longitudinal Research*. Boston: Martinus Nijhoff Publishing.

Scottish Education Department (1979) *Health Education in Primary, Secondary and Special Schools in Scotland*. Edinburgh: HMSO.

Scottish Health Education Group (1985) *Drugs and Young People in Scotland*. Edinburgh: Scottish Health Education Group.

Scottish Health Education Unit (1970) *Health Education and Alcohol*. Scottish Health Service Studies No. 14. Edinburgh: Scottish Home and Health Department.

Scottish Home and Health Department (1981) *Criminal Statistics Scotland 1979*. Edinburgh: HMSO.

—— (1981) (Personal communication).

—— (1984) Figures supplied from Criminal Statistics by Criminal Statistics Unit, Edinburgh. (Personal communication.)

180 Alcohol, Drugs, and School-leavers

Scottish Office (1979) *Drunken Offenders in Scotland*. Edinburgh: Scottish Office.

Seabrook, J. (1982) *Unemployment*. London: Paladin.

Semple, B. M. and Yarrow, A. (1974) Health Education, Alcohol and Alcoholism in Scotland. *Health Bulletin* XXXII, 1: 1–4.

Shaw, S. J. (1980) The Causes of Increasing Drinking Problems amongst Women. In Camberwell Council on Alcoholism (eds) *Women and Alcohol*. London: Tavistock.

Shephard, R. J. (1982) *The Risks of Passive Smoking*. London: Croom Helm.

Showler, B. and Sinfield, A. (1981) *The Workless State*. Oxford: Martin Robertson.

Simpura, J. (1978) *Drinking Practices of the Finnish Population in 1969 and 1976. Used Quantities and Problem Drinking. Report No. 114*. Helsinki: Social Research Institute of Alcohol Studies.

—— (1984) Comment made in discussion of these results at Alcohol Epidemiology Symposium, ICAA, Edinburgh.

Sinfield, A. (1981) *What Unemployment Means*. Oxford: Martin Robertson.

Singh, A. (1979) Reliability and Validity of Self-Reported Delinquency Studies. *Psychological Reports* 44: 987–93.

Single, E., Morgan, P., and de Lint, J. (eds) (1981) *Alcohol, Society and the State. 2: The Social History of Control Policy in Seven Countries*. Toronto: Addiction Research Foundation.

Skog, O.-J. (1979) *Drinking Behaviour in Small Groups: The Relationship between Group Size and Consumption Level*. Oslo: Statens Institut for Alkoholforskning.

Smart, R. G. (1976a) *The New Drinkers: Teenage Use and Abuse of Alcohol*. Toronto: Addiction Research Foundation, Programme Report Series No. 4.

—— (1976b) Spontaneous Recovery in Alcoholics: A Review of the Evidence. *Drug and Alcohol Dependence* 1: 277–85.

—— (1979a) Priorities in Minimizing Alcohol Problems among Young People. In H. T. Blane and M. E. Chafetz (eds) *Youth, Alcohol and Social Policy*. New York: Plenum.

—— (1979b) Young Alcoholics in Treatment: Their Characteristics and Recovery Rates at Follow-up. *Alcoholism: Clinical and Experimental Research* 3,1: 19–23.

—— (1980) Some Recent Studies of Teenage Alcoholism and Problem Drinking. *Phenomenology and Treatment of Alcoholism* Spectrum: 127–38.

Smart, R. G. and Blair, N. L. (1980) Drug Use and Drug Problems among Teenagers in a Household Sample. *Drug and Alcohol Dependence* 5: 171–79.

Smart, R. G. and Fejer, D. C. (1974) *Drug Education: Current Issues. Future Directions*. Toronto: Addiction Research Foundation.

Smart, R. G., Arif, A., Hughes, P., Mora, M. E., Navaratnam, V., Varma, V. K., and Wadud, K. A. (1981) *Drug Use Among Non-Student Youth*. Offset Publication No. 60. Geneva: World Health Organisation.

Smart, R. G., Gray, G., and Bennett, C. (1978) Predictors of Drinking and Signs of Heavy Drinking among High School Students. *International Journal of the Addictions* 13, 7: 1079–94.

Smart, R. G. and Liban, C. B. (1980) Cannabis Use and Alcohol Problems among Adults and Students. *Drug and Alcohol Dependence* 6: 141–47.

—— (1981) Predictors of Problem Drinking among Elderly, Middle-aged and Youthful Drinkers. *Journal of Psychoactive Drugs* 13, 2: 153–63.

Smart, R. G. and Murray, G. E. (1981) A Review of Trends in Alcohol and Cannabis Use among Young People. *Bulletin on Narcotics* XXXIII, 4: 77–90.

—— (1983) Drug Abuse and Affluence in Five Countries: A Study of Economic and Health Conditions, 1960–1975. *Drug and Alcohol Dependence* 11: 297–307.

Smart, R. G., Mora, M.-E., Terroba, G., and Varma, V. K. (1981) Drug Use among Non-Students in Three Countries. *Drug and Alcohol Dependence* 7: 125–32.

Smith, R. (1981) Alcohol, Women and the Young: The Same Old Problem? *British Medical Journal* 283: 1170–1172.

Snyder, C. R. (1978) *Alcohol and the Jews.* USA: Arctivus Paperbacks.

Sobell, L. and Sobell, M. (1978) Validity of Self-Reports in Three Populations of Alcoholics. *Journal of Consulting and Clinical Psychology* 46: 901–7.

Spear, H. B. (1983) Drug Abuse and Deaths. *British Journal of Addiction* 78, 2: 173–80.

Spiegler, D. L. (1983) Children's Attitudes to Alcohol. *Journal of Studies on Alcohol* 44, 3: 545–52.

Stacey, B. G. (1981) *Alcohol and Youth in New Zealand.* Christchurch: Psychology Department, University of Canterbury.

Stacey, B. G. and Elvy, G. A. (1981) Is Alcohol Consumption Log-Normally Distributed among Fourteen to Seventeen Year Olds? *Psychological Reports* 48: 995–1005.

Stimson, G. V. (1973) *Heroin and Behaviour.* Shannon: Irish University Press.

—— (1981) Epidemiological Research on Drug Use in General Populations. In G. Edwards and C. Busch (eds) *Drug Problems in Britain.* London: Academic Press.

Stimson, G. V. and Oppenheimer, E. (1982) *Heroin Addiction.* London: Tavistock.

Straus, R. and Bacon, S. D. (1953) *Drinking in College.* New Haven, Conn.: Yale University Press.

Stumphauzer, J. S. (1980) Learning to Drink: Adolescents and Alcohol, *Addictive Behaviours* 5: 277–83.

——(1982) Learning to Drink. II. Peer Survey of Normal Adolescents. *International Journal of the Addictions* 17, 8: 1363–372.

Sulkunen, P. (1979) *Abstainers in Finland 1946–1976. Report No. 133.* Helsinki: Social Research Institute of Alcohol Studies.

—— (1981) *The Wet Generation, Living Conditions and Drinking Patterns in Finland. Continuities in a Reanalysis of Finnish Drinking Survey Data. Report No. 155.* Helsinki: Social Research Institute of Alcohol Studies.

Taylor, D. (1981) *Alcohol: Reducing the Harm.* London: Office of Health Economics.

Taylor, I., Walton, P., and Young, J. (eds) (1975) *Critical Criminology.* London: Routledge & Kegan Paul.

Taylor, P. (1984) *Smoke Ring: The Politics of Tobacco.* London: Bodley Head.

Thompson, E. L. (1978) Smoking Education Programs 1960–1976. *American Journal of Public Health* 68, 3: 250–51.

Thorley, A. (1981) Longitudinal Studies of Drug Dependence. In G. Edwards and C. Busch (eds) *Drug Problems in Britain*. London: Academic Press.

—— (1982) The Effects of Alcohol. In M. A. Plant (ed.) *Drinking and Problem Drinking*. London: Junction.

—— (1983) (Personal communication).

Thorley, A. and Plant, M. A. (1982) Misuse of Drugs. In R. G. McCreadie (ed.) *Rehabilitation in Psychiatric Practice*. London: Pitman.

Tobacco Advisory Council (1984) Estimated public consumption of tobacco goods in the United Kingdom. Cited in *General Household Survey 1982*. London: Office of Population Censuses and Surveys (1984), 189.

Townsend, P. and Davidson, N. (1982) *Inequalities in Health*. Harmondsworth: Pelican. (The Black Report.)

Trotter, T. (1813) *An Essay, Medical, Philosophical and Chemical on Drunkenness, and its Effects on the Human Body* (republished 1981). Boston: Bradford and Read.

Tuchfield, B. S. (1981) Spontaneous Remission in Alcoholics: Empirical Observations in Theoretical Implications. *Journal of Studies on Alcohol* 42: 626–41.

United States Department of Health, Education, and Welfare (1978) *Alcohol and Health: Third Special Report to Congress*. Washington, DC: US Government Printing Office.

Vaillant, G. E. (1983a) *The Natural History of Alcoholism*. Cambridge, Mass.: Harvard University Press.

—— (1983b) Natural History of Male Alcoholism. V. Is Alcoholism the Cart or the Horse to Sociopathy? *British Journal of Addiction* 78, 3: 317–26.

Vingilis, E. and Smart, R. G. (1981) Physical Dependence on Alcohol in Youth. In Y. Israel, F. B. Glaser, H. Kalant, R. E. Popham, W. Schmidt, and R. G. Smart *Research Advances in Alcohol and Drug Problems. Vol. 6*. New York: Plenum.

Virtanen, M. (1981) *The Generativity of Education. The 'Moderation Rules OK' Campaign considered as Part of ALKO Policy*. Helsinki: Social Research Institute of Alcohol Studies.

Vissing, Y. M. (1978) How Do the Schools View Substance Education and Prevention? *Journal of Drug Education* 8, 4: 267–77.

Wagenaar, A. (1981) Effects of the Raised Legal Drinking Age on Motor Vehicle Accidents in Michigan. *HSRI Research Review* 111: 1–8.

Waldorf, D. (1973) *Careers in Dope*. Englewood Cliffs, NJ: Prentice-Hall.

Walker, B. A., Jasinka, M. D., and Carnes, E. F. (1978) Adolescent Alcohol Abuse: A Review of the Literature. *Journal of Alcohol and Drug Education* 23: 51–65.

Wallack, L. (1982) *Prevention: A Point of Departure*. Berkeley: Alcohol Research Group (mimeograph).

Walsh, B. M. (1980) *Drinking in Ireland*. Dublin: Economic and Social Research Unit. Broadsheet No. 20.

Waring, M. L., Petraglia, G., Cohen, L., and Busby, E. (1984) Alcohol Use Patterns of Graduate Students in Social Work and on Business. *Journal of Studies on Alcohol* 45, 3: 268–71.

Warr, P., Jackson, P., and Banks, M. (1982) Duration of Unemployment and

Psychological Well-Being in Young Men and Women. *Current Psychological Research* 2: 207–14.

Wechsler, H. (1979) Patterns of Alcohol Consumption among the Young: High School, College and General Population Studies. In H. T. Blane and M. E. Chafetz (eds) *Youth, Alcohol and Social Policy*. New York: Plenum.

Wechsler, H., Demoine, H. W., Jnr, and Gottleils, N. (1978) Drinking Patterns of Greater Boston Adults: Subgroup Differences on the QFV Index. *Journal of Studies on Alcohol* 39: 1158–165.

Wechsler, H. and McFadden, M. (1979) Drinking among College Students in New England: Extent, Social Correlates and Consequences of Alcohol Use. *Journal of Studies on Alcohol* 40: 969–96.

Wechsler, H. and Rohman, R. E. (1981) Extensive Users of Alcohol among College Students. *Journal of Studies on Alcohol* 42: 149–55.

Wechsler, H. and Thum, D. (1973) Teenage Drinking, Drug Use and Social Correlates. *Quarterly Journal of Studies on Alcohol* 34, 4: 1220–227.

Weir, R. B. (1984) Obsessed with Moderation: The Drink Trades and the Drink Question (1870–1930). *British Journal of Addiction* 79: 93–107.

Wiener, R. S. P. (1970) *Drugs and Schoolchildren*. London: Longman.

Williams, A., Zador, P., Harris, S., and Karpf, R. (1982) The Effect of Raising the Legal Minimum Drinking Age on Fatal Crash Involvement. *Journal of Legal Studies* cited by Ross (1984).

Williams, G. P. and Brake, G. T. (1980) *Drink in Great Britain 1900 to 1979*. London: Edsall.

——(1982) *The English Public House in Transition*. London: Edsall.

Willis, J. H. (1969) The Natural History of Drug Dependence: Some Comparative Observations on United Kingdom and United States Subjects. In H. Steinberg (ed.) *Scientific Basis of Drug Dependence*. London: Churchill.

Wilsnack, R. W. and Wilsnack, S. C. (1980) Drinking and Denial of Social Obligations among Adolescent Boys. *Journal of Studies on Alcohol* 41, 11: 1118–33.

Wilson, G. B. (1940) *Alcohol and the Nation*. London: Nicholson and Watson.

Wilson, P. (1980a) *Drinking in England and Wales*. London: HMSO.

—— (1980b) Drinking Habits in the United Kingdom. *Population Trends* 22, Winter: 14–18.

World Health Organisation (1977) *Alcohol-Related Disabilities* (Offset Publication No. 32). Geneva: WHO.

——(1979) *Controlling the Smoking Epidemic*. Technical Report Series 636. Geneva: WHO.

Wright, J. D. and Pearl, L. (1981) Knowledge and Experience of Young People Regarding Drug Abuse between 1969 and 1979. *British Medical Journal* 282, 7 March: 793–96.

Young, J. (1971) *The Drugtakers*. London: Paladin.

Zacune, J. and Hensman, C. (1971) *Drugs, Alcohol and Tobacco in Britain*. London: Heinemann Medical.

Zucker, R. A. and Harford, T. C. (1983) National Study of the Demography of Adolescent Drinking Practices. *Journal of Studies on Alcohol* 44, 6: 974–85.

Name Index

Subject Index